Revelation's
GREAT
LOVE STORY

Other books by Larry L. Lichtenwalter:

Behind the Seen: God's Hand in Esther's Life . . . and Yours
David: A Heart Like His (The Shepherd Years)
David: Faith on the Run (The Fugitive Years)
David: Dancing Like a King (The Royal Years)
Out of the Pit: Joseph's Story and Yours
Well-driven Nails
Wrestling With Angels

To order, call **1-800-765-6955.**

Visit us at **www.AutumnHousePublishing.com**
for information on other Autumn House® products.

Revelation's GREAT LOVE STORY

MORE THAN I EVER IMAGINED

LARRY L. LICHTENWALTER

Autumn House® Publishing
www.autumnhousepublishing.com
A Division of **REVIEW AND HERALD® PUBLISHING**
Since 1861

Published by Autumn House® Publishing, a division of Review and Herald® Publishing, Hagerstown, MD 21741-1119

Autumn House® titles may be purchased in bulk for educational, business, fund-raising, or sales promotional use. For information, please e-mail SpecialMarkets@reviewandherald.com.

Autumn House® Publishing publishes biblically based materials for spiritual, physical, and mental growth and Christian discipleship.

The author assumes full responsibility for the accuracy of all facts and quotations as cited in this book.

Scripture quotations marked NASB are from the *New American Standard Bible,* copyright © 1960, 1962, 1963, 1968, 1971, 1972, 1973, 1975, 1977, 1994 by The Lockman Foundation. Used by permission.

Texts credited to NEB are from *The New English Bible.* © The Delegates of the Oxford University Press and the Syndics of the Cambridge University Press 1961, 1970. Reprinted by permission.

Texts credited to NIV are from the *Holy Bible, New International Version.* Copyright © 1973, 1978, 1984, International Bible Society. Used by permission of Zondervan Bible Publishers.

Texts credited to NKJV are from the New King James Version. Copyright © 1979, 1980, 1982 by Thomas Nelson, Inc. Used by permission. All rights reserved.

Scripture quotations marked NLT are taken from the *Holy Bible,* New Living Translation, copyright © 1996. Used by permission of Tyndale House Publishers, Inc., Wheaton, Illinois 60189. All rights reserved.

Bible texts credited to TEV are from the *Good News Bible*—Old Testament: Copyright © American Bible Society 1976, 1992; New Testament: Copyright © American Bible Society 1966, 1971, 1976, 1992.

Verses marked TLB are taken from *The Living Bible,* copyright © 1971 by Tyndale House Publishers, Wheaton, Ill. Used by permission.

This book was
Edited by Gerald Wheeler
Copyedited by James Cavil
Cover designed by Trent Truman
Cover image by: © Bluestocking, Beltsazardaniel, EduardHarkonen/istockphoto.com. Digital composite.
Interior designed by Heather Rogers
Typeset: Bembo 11/13

PRINTED IN U.S.A.
12 11 10 09 08   5 4 3 2 1

Library of Congress Cataloging-in-Publication Data
Lichtenwalter, Larry L
   Revelation's great love story: more than I ever imagined / Larry L. Lichtenwalter.
   p. cm.
1. Bible. N.T. Revelation—Criticism, interpretation, etc. 2. Adventists—Doctrines. I. Title.
BS2825.52.L53 2007
228'.06—dc22
                              2007004912

ISBN 978-0-8127-0460-0

DEDICATION

To my sons
Erich, Ehren, Ethan, Evan, and Steaven

So they will never forget why I love Jesus,
Why they can love Him, too,
And how we can experience His love together through eternity

CONTENTS

INTRODUCTION

Some Things You Never Forget

One of the things I learned the summer that my father died was that there are some things you never forget. The decades can steal your strength, but not your memory. The seasons may wrinkle your face, but they don't soften certain feelings or attitudes, hurts or sorrows, privileges or blessings. One thing my father never forgot was rejection. He remembered being abused as a child, his horrific experiences as a teenage soldier in the South Pacific theater during World War II, and a host of other blistering moments throughout his adult life. As a 70-year-old dying of painful leukemia, he could still see and feel them. People. Events. Injustices. Resentments. Failures. Painful realities that he found himself compelled to talk to me about in hopes of finding closure—peace. He wanted to die with his heart filled with the quiet and meaning that had always seemed to elude him throughout his turbulent life.

John couldn't forget Jesus. More than 60 years had passed, but the prophet saw Jesus still. The decades had taken his strength, but they hadn't stolen his memory of Jesus. While time had dulled his sight, it hadn't blurred his vision of Jesus. He had been with Jesus, Jesus had been with him, and how could John ever forget? He had been there, with Jesus.[1]

John was the disciple Jesus loved (John 13:23; 19:26; 20:2; 21:7, 20). He seems to have enjoyed a deeper, more personal relationship with Him than the other apostles did. While Jesus loved all the disciples, John appar-

9

ently had the most receptive spirit. He opened his heart and yielded himself to Christ more fully. Although he was just a young person at the time, something connected between him and Jesus that forever changed his life.[2] One of the hotheaded "sons of thunder" (Mark 3:17; cf. Luke 9:54), he experienced the love of Jesus and became so much like Him that the love of Jesus, loving Jesus, and loving others became his passion—the theme of his life and ministry. Having once experienced the love of Jesus, he forever wanted to talk about how much Jesus loved him and how much Jesus loves everyone. The disciple never forgot the Jesus he had learned to love. Jesus was all that he wanted to talk about and live for.

I can imagine him as an old man wondering, *What about those who will not see or hear or touch Jesus? How can they ever speak of someone they have never seen? How can they ever explain words they have never heard? How can they ever believe? What will happen when I, John, am gone? How will others know? If only they could have been there. If only they could have seen Jesus for themselves.* And so we find the disciple under the inspiration of the Holy Spirit writing about Jesus 60-plus years later. In fact, he composed three books: the Apocalypse (Revelation), a collection of three short little letters (the Epistles of John), and a Gospel (John)—possibly in that order. It's as if he is saying, "This is the Jesus I know. The Jesus you can know. Here is why I love Jesus—why you also can love Him. Hear Him. Touch Him. Do that, and you can love Him just as I do" (see 1 John 1:1-4).

Three Books About Loving Jesus

John's Gospel is about loving Jesus! It unfolds God's incredible love for us—"For God so loved the world," it exclaims (John 3:16; cf. 1:17; 5:42). Allowing us to behold Christ's self-sacrificing love, it invites us personally to experience His atoning work in our behalf (John 1:11-14; 11:3, 5; 13:1, 23, 34; 15:9, 10; 20:7, 20). Then it invites us to passionately love Jesus in return—to literally "abide" in His love (John 15:9, 10; 14:15, 24, 28). Finally it exhorts us to display the kind of love for one another that Jesus has shown us, thus manifesting His love in all our interpersonal relationships (John 13:34, 35; 15:12, 13, 17). "Do you love Me?" Jesus asked Peter point blank one early morning on a Galilean shore (John 21:15, 16, 17). And it's the question that He still confronts each one of us with—"Do you love Me?"

John's three little letters are also about loving Jesus. They tell of seeing, hearing, touching, and being with Him. The disciple wrote them so that we in faith can also see Jesus, hear Jesus, and touch Him, too! So that our joy can be full in the experience and sharing of intimate loving fellowship with both the Father and Son (1 John 1:1-4). "See how great a love the Father has bestowed on us," he tells us, "that we would be called children of God" (1 John 3:1, NASB). "God is love" (1 John 4:8, 16), and He has manifested His awesome love by sending His only Son into the world as a propitiation for our sins so that we might live through Him (verses 9, 10). And so "we love [God], because he first loved us" (verse 19). Then "if God so loved us [and we truly love Him], we ought also to love one another" (verse 11; cf. 2 John 5).

Like his Gospel, John's letters unfold the practical link between our love for Jesus and our love for one another (1 John 3:10-17; 4:10-19). True love will ever display itself in word and deed (1 John 3:18). "May grace, mercy, and peace, which come from God our Father and from Jesus Christ his Son, be with us who live in truth and love," he writes to a woman held in high esteem (2 John 3, NLT). In other words, we live in the sphere of divine love, and so we too love—Jesus.

John's Apocalypse—the book of Revelation—is about loving Jesus! We don't normally (or naturally) think about the love of Jesus or of a "loving Jesus" when we read Revelation. Many of us read the Apocalypse with forebodings rather than hope. It produces in us ethical confusion rather than certainty, or moral disdain rather than passion. The book's beasts and blasphemy, battles and blood, and destruction, despair, and darkness quickly overwhelm us. Revelation's violent sequences of war and threats of judgment and eternal damnation make the book a challenging, often horrifying, bewildering, and confusing text.[3] Some of us wonder if we need the apocalyptic vision that Revelation presents because of the moral stance it appears to engender.[4] The book elicits strong reactions—both positive and negative.

But John opens Revelation with a phrase that unfolds both the title and subject of the book: "the revelation of Jesus Christ" (Rev. 1:1).[5] It tells the story of the whole book in a nutshell[6]—Jesus! The word "revelation" comes from the Greek *apokalupsis* ("apocalypse"), which means "unveiling," or "revealing." But in our contemporary culture the term "Apocalypse" has become a synonym for "doomsday," a reference to the end of the world, whether by violence, economic catastrophe, or natural disaster.[7] But for John and his readers, the Apocalypse was a revealing of Jesus Christ—an unveiling of His greatness and glory,[8] of which Jesus Christ is both the *content* and *agent* of this revealing.[9]

It follows then that the book of Revelation is, in the first place, not information about the bad world we live in and the horrible events to come, or a report on the first-century church under persecution. Nor is it an outline of end-time events. Rather, it is about Jesus, Scripture's last word on Him.[10] It presents Jesus Christ as history's controlling reality and describes Him in such a way that absolutely everything is subordinated to Him.[11]

Revelation is nothing if not focused on Jesus Christ. Sustaining this focus will ever be our challenge. Our attention easily wanders as we find so many fascinating symbols to pursue and so many intriguing subjects to explore. Sensational applications easily captivate our imagination. Other things in the book may disturb and disgust us. It is easy to let Jesus drift from the center of our reading.

♪ Jesus Loves Me

The most important thing that we must always keep in mind is that the Jesus of the Apocalypse loves us deeply. "To him who loves us," John writes with overflowing, doxological praise in the book's prologue, "to Him *be* the glory and the dominion forever and ever. Amen" (Rev. 1:5, 6, NASB). The form of the verb John uses for "love" is a present active participle (avgapw/nti) that depicts love as something current, continuous, compelling, and real. It is love that encompasses our past, our present, and our every tomorrow.[12]

Most wonderful (and surprising) of all, we are the privileged objects of Jesus' incredible love! He loves you and me—every one of us. Before we hear anything else, whether it be about the seven churches or seals, the dragon chasing the woman into the wilderness, the Lamb and the 144,000 standing on Mount Zion, or the meaning of 666, John first wants to tell us that Jesus loves us (Rev. 1:5). Revelation unequivocally declares that He loves you and me!

♪ Appearing as it does in the book's prologue, Jesus' love for us is one of the significant themes that sets the tone for the entire Apocalypse and subtly wends its way through each unfolding vision. Introductions are important. They not only gain attention and draw the reader/hearer into the story or text; they also unfold its theme(s) and prepare the audience for understanding what lies ahead. The content of an introduction clarifies purpose and holds out promise of what the "take away" from hearing the story or reading an essay will be. Like a good story or literary piece, Revelation's introduction (and conclusion) is crammed with meaning and gives a viewpoint on the whole book that greatly facilitates its interpretation. If we want to know where Revelation is headed and what it intends to do to us, we must listen carefully to its beginning (and ending). That Jesus loves us, and that He has already demonstrated His love for us (released us from our sins by His shed blood), is key to everything else we encounter in the book.

Did you know that it is only because Jesus passionately loves us that He comes to us with words of commendation or condemnation, assurance and assistance? He is threatening, blunt, directive, inviting, and hope-filled because He loves us. That's what Revelation's imagery of Jesus walking among the seven lampstands (seven churches) is all about—a caring Jesus who loves us (Rev. 1:12-3:21). "Those whom I love, I reprove and discipline," He maintains (Rev. 3:19, NASB). And did you know that Jesus promises that at some future time it will be clear to everyone who lives here on earth that He does love us (see Rev. 3:9)? Sometimes we wonder. The world around us frequently gives us a quite different impression. Often it doesn't look as if it matters at all whether we remain faithful or not. But Jesus says, Just hang in there and see. When I bring you through in the end, it will be clear to everyone that I loved you (Rev. 3:9, 10; cf. Ps. 73:1-26).

While the book doesn't specifically refer to Jesus' love once it gets past the narrative of His activity among the seven churches, the theme nevertheless wends its way subtly through each unfolding vision and is everywhere assumed and operative in the Apocalypse.[13] It is implicit in the vision of the slain Lamb whose blood has ransomed people for God from every tribe and language and people and nation and to whom adoring angels ascribe worth (Rev. 5:9, 10, 12). The imagery of divine protective sealing and blood-bleached white robes that enable the redeemed both to go through the coming great tribulation and to stand triumphant when Christ appears in the clouds of glory takes such love for granted (Rev. 7:1-3, 9, 10, 14; 6:17; cf. 3:10). And it is understood in the divine response to the heart-wrenching prayer of the saints (Rev. 6:10; 5:8; 8:1-4) and the sovereign protection for those whom the serpent pursues to destroy (Rev. 12:6, 14-16).

Christ's love stands behind the reality of the three-pronged gospel warning to every nation, tribe, tongue and people (Rev. 14:6-12). That same love invites the honest in heart to come out of Babylon while there's still time (Rev. 18:4). It provides opportunity for everyone to become a personal guest at the Lamb's wedding banquet (Rev. 19:9). And it cries out above the demonic gathering of the world for Armageddon's battle with the exhortation to stay awake and keep one's clothes on so that no one will not run around naked and be ashamed when Jesus returns (Rev. 16:15).

Revelation's Great Love Story

Then near Revelation's close we once again catch a clear reference to a love everywhere assumed and operative in the book. At the conclusion of the millennium an innumerable multitude from the four corners of the earth—Gog and Magog—gather one last time to destroy God's people. They assemble on the broad plain of the earth and surround the camp of the saints—the beloved city (Rev. 20:9). The language naturally equates the two: the camp of the saints and the Beloved City (i.e., "the camp of the saints, even the Beloved City"). They are one and the same. The city is loved because the people dwelling there are loved. The city, after all, is the Lamb's bride (Rev. 21:2, 9, 10).

Revelation's final scenes likewise sum up Christ's love for us. We find a new heaven and a new earth (Rev. 21:1). God Himself now dwells among His people, wiping away their tears and forever removing all that wounds (verses 3, 4). The river of life flows from the divine throne, and the tree of life has leaves that heal the alienation of nations (Rev. 22:1, 2). No curse of any kind threatens the universe (verse 3). The redeemed see the face of God, finally, unveiled (verse 4). And the book promises that Jesus will return—quickly, in fact (verses 12, 20). God offers access to the tree of life and to the Holy City (verse 14).

Here too, we find an invitation—to come to God before our characters have become fixed (verse 11) and opportunity yet remains (verse 17). Here Jesus affirms that He is the personal source of all the hope and help unfolded in the Apocalypse (verse 16). He is the source of David and the heir to his throne, the bright morning star that will awaken the dawn of eternity, forever ending the long black night of terror and suffering (verse 16; cf. 2 Peter 1:19). And it is the "grace" of the Lord Jesus that the Apocalypse presents as its final thought to every reader—as if to say, "This is what this revealing of Jesus is all about. Grace. Let it hang on your lips and haunt your imagination" (see verse 21). It is grace flowing from a heart that loves us dearly—Jesus.

Again, if we want to know where the book of Revelation is headed and what it intends to do to us, we must listen carefully to its beginning and ending—that Jesus loves us. It is key to everything we read in the book.

Do You Love Me?

In the process of closing, Revelation becomes more personal—intensely personal, in fact. The book shifts from the cosmic to the individual, from global events and world history to personal accountability and inner-world decisions, and from apocalyptic visions to private vision. By doing so, Revelation no longer speaks to just everyone. Now it focuses on the one (verse 17)—to you and to me individually. Ultimately each one of us must see how much Jesus loves us and respond personally to that incredible love. Thus Revelation not only tells us how much Jesus loves us, but also calls us to love Him in return. When we see who Jesus is and all that He has done, is doing, and will do, we cannot help loving Him in return.

"Do you love Me?" is one of the first things Jesus Himself wonders as He speaks to Ephesus, the first of the seven Asian churches to which the Apocalypse is addressed. "Your first love? Is it still there?" He asks. "Do you still love me? I know all about you—your hard work and your patient endurance. I know your theological integrity and how you don't tolerate evil people but are a bastian of orthodoxy. An active and aggressive congregation, you are a veritable beehive of industry. I know how you have patiently suffered for me without quitting. But I have *this* complaint against you. You don't love me as you did at first," He observes (see verse 4).

Neil Diamond and Barbra Streisand recorded a song that starts out with her singing, "You don't bring me flowers." They go on to lament that things have changed. Their love having grown cold, they just shut off the lights at night with no kissing, affection, or lovemaking. Now they're like two ships passing in the night. So they end with "You don't say you need me" and "You don't bring me flowers anymore." Such are the words of lovers whose love has grown cold. It's powerful imagery that reminds me of another pop song that announces that the singer loves someone more today than yesterday but less than they will tomorrow. Sounds wonderful, doesn't it? More love today than yesterday. Less love today than tomorrow? But can it be true? How often does it really happen? Isn't human experience often more like less love today than yesterday, and more love today than tomorrow?

That's what Jesus was sensing was the case with Ephesus. It was a splendid congregation. A model church, its members were busy in their service, patient in their sufferings and labors, and orthodox in their belief. What more could anyone ask of them? Just one thing—*love*. They toiled with vigor and endured with fortitude, but without love. And when they tested their teachers with orthodoxy, they had no love in their hearts.[14] "Without love, everything is nothing."[15] You've left your first love, Jesus says. While you're doing all the right things, something is still missing. You simply don't love Me the same way anymore.

If we're honest with ourselves, we know deep down inside that He's probably right—even about us as well! Some of us work hard for God, enduring much for His name. Not yet grown weary, we're orthodox and discerning, holding people accountable. God's Word and truth are important. But something is missing. The romance (spiritual passion) is gone, or it's just not the same. The routine has replaced our first love. With our minds absorbed with other things, our spiritual life has become dull and dry and maybe empty. Perhaps we've even become tired of the empty routines of worship, Bible study, devotions, and perhaps even God Himself. Maybe we're not really sure that we love Jesus, or that He does indeed love us.

J Have we lost our first love? Do we love Jesus more or less today than yesterday? How about tomorrow? Will we love Him more then? That's what Jesus wonders. And that's what Revelation is all about. In it He yearns for a people who are "with him [the Lamb]" as the called, the chosen, and the faithful—not out of expediency, but love (Rev. 17:14). In it He describes a people who "follow the Lamb wherever He goes"—not out of blind obedience, but love (Rev. 14:4, NASB). There He tells of those who "did not love their life when faced with death"—not out of promise for great reward, but because they passionately love Him who gave His life for them (Rev. 12:11). His eye is on those who faithfully endure under great trial—not out of principle alone, but because it is for Him that they love to live and to obey (Rev. 14:12; cf. 12:17). There, too, He shakes the objects of His love from their halfheartedness to wholehearted love for Him (Rev. 3:14-18). He lingers at the heart's door, gently knocking in order to awaken love (verses 19, 20). As with the love of Jesus for us, our love for Him is everywhere assumed in the Apocalypse. Why else would Christ's bride adorn herself and make herself ready for His grand appearing, but out of passionate love for Him (see Rev. 19:7, 8; 21:2)?

Oh, Yes, I Love Jesus

Dietrich Bonhoeffer was only 39 when the Nazis hanged him at the Flossenberg prison for being part of the underground working for Hitler's defeat. Just a relatively young Lutheran pastor, he nevertheless understood the essence of "first love." In his moving book *The Cost of Discipleship* we read these poignant words: "Besides Jesus nothing has any significance. He alone matters. When we are called to follow Christ, we are summoned to an exclusive attachment to his person."[16]

Revelation unfolds the "person of Jesus" with such vivid imagery that our hearts will welcome such exclusive attachment. He alone will matter. We will respond to His call to follow with a heart full of love.

"Do you love Me?" Jesus still asks us. One of the choruses young people like to sing raises that same question: "Oh, friend, do you love Jesus?" "Oh, yes, I love Jesus" is the ready reply. "Then why do you love Jesus?" it presses further. "Here's why I love Jesus" comes the answer: "because He first loved me." Thus this book. I love Jesus because He first loved me in the way this last book of Scripture vividly portrays, and thus no one else could ever draw me into such exclusive attachment as Jesus. May your journey through these pages on Revelation so fill your imagination with Jesus that your heart, too, will overflow with love for Him.

---

[1] Max Lucado, ed., *Life Lessons From the Inspired Word of God: Book of John* (Dallas: Word Publishing, 1996), pp. 9, 10.

[2] See Ellen G. White, *The Acts of the Apostles* (Mountain View, Calif.: Pacific Press Pub. Assn., 1911), pp. 539, 544, 545.

[3] Harry O. Maier, *Apocalypse Recalled: The Book of Revelation After Christendom* (Minneapolis: Fortress Press, 2002), p. ix.

[4] Beatrice Neall, "Apocalyptic—Who Needs It?" *Spectrum* 23, no. 1 (May 1993): 46.

[5] Craig S. Keener, *The NIV Application Commentary: Revelation* (Grand Rapids: Zondervan Pub. House, 2000), p. 53.

[6] Robert L. Thomas, *Revelation 1-7: An Exegetical Commentary* (Chicago: Moody Press, 1992), p. 50.

[7] Jon Paulien, "The Lion/Lamb King: Reading the Apocalypse From Popular Culture," in *Reading the Book of Revelation: A Resource for Students*, ed. David L. Barr (Atlanta: Society of Biblical Literature, 2003), pp. 152-154.

[8] John R. W. Stott, *The Incomparable Christ* (Downers Grove, Ill.: InterVarsity Press, 2001), p. 173.

[9] Eugene H. Peterson, *Reversed Thunder: The Revelation of John and the Praying Imagination* (New York: Harper San Francisco, 1988), p. 26.

[10] *Ibid.*, p. 26.

[11] *Ibid.*, pp. 27, 28.

[12] Grant R. Osborne, *Revelation* (Grand Rapids: Baker Academic, 2002), p. 64.

[13] *Ibid.*

[14] John R. W. Stott, *What Christ Thinks of the Church* (Grand Rapids: William B. Eerdmans Pub. Co., 1958), pp. 23-28.

[15] Stott, *The Incomparable Christ*, p. 178.

[16] Dietrich Bonhoeffer, *The Cost of Discipleship*, p. 63.

HE'S BIGGER THAN I AM

Famous Last Words
Revelation 1:9-18

It was a colossal enterprise involving more than 1 million square feet of shimmering aluminum-colored fabric, 90 specially trained rock climbers, 10 miles of bright blue polypropylene rope, 220 tons of steel structure, and 120 construction workers. And 24 years of planning and negotiating. Tailored as carefully as a dress and billowing in the wind, it was a work of art, a cultural event, a political happening, and an ambitious piece of business. The cost? A fat $10 million. All to wrap Berlin's historic century-old Reichstag building. But it was a dream come true for Christo Javacheff and his wife Jeanne-Claude. The New York artist couple spend their time creating art on a monumental scale by temporarily transforming natural or human-made landmarks with fabric. Their purpose is to so alter the familiar so that it is seen anew, turning it into something that we can no longer take for granted or overlook.

I had a midnight tour around the "Wrapped Reichstag." The Reichstag is an immense stone hulk, a heavy and stolid building from the nineteenth century. But there against the night sky and bathed by spotlights all around, it looked light, almost delicate, as if it could float away. It shimmered where it was once solid. And it was refined where it was once unattractive. The wrapping brought a transforming image to a building that had lost its mystique for the German people. For years following World War II it lay a bombed-out shell. But the wrapping forced the eye to confront the Reichstag anew. By stirring the imagination, it helped to bring the Reichstag back into the mainstream of Berlin, where it now, fully renovated with modern furnishings and services, once again houses Germany's Parliament.[1]

Like the old Reichstag, Jesus can become so familiar to us that, unless we take pains, we hardly see Him anymore. Unless Jesus is wrapped in a way that forces the eye to view Him differently, we will go on in our luke-warmness and satisfaction with the lesser things of this world. Thus Revelation presents a transforming vision of Jesus. One that enables us to see Jesus in a new way that can both awaken spiritual life and draw us into an ever deepening sense of His presence. It's a vision that can awaken our love for Him.

In Revelation 1:9-11 John sets the scene for his first glimpse of Jesus in more than 60 years. Sentenced to exile on the island of Patmos, one day he found himself "in the Spirit" as the Holy Spirit took hold of him. Then, before he saw Jesus, he heard His voice—loud and peremptory, behind him, like the blast of a trumpet. It commanded to write down what he was about to see, and to send it to the seven churches of the Roman province of Asia, beginning with Ephesus, the capital and the nearest to Patmos, and continuing north and then southeast on the circular road that linked them all together.

When he turned around to see whose voice it was, John first had his attention caught by seven golden lampstands. They were only the frame-work of the scene, however. Much more important was the person stand-ing in their midst. The person John sees has human form—one "like a son of man" (verse 13, NIV). Yet He is a commanding, glorious, and divine figure dressed in a long robe that reaches down to His feet and is secured by a golden sash around His chest. They are the kind of garments a king, a priest, or a judge would wear. "His head and His hair were white like white wool, like snow; and His eyes were like a flame of fire. His feet were like burnished bronze, when it has been made to glow in a furnace, and His voice was like the sound of many waters. In His right hand He held seven stars, and out of His mouth came a sharp two-edged sword; and His face was like the sun shining in its strength" (verses 14-16, NASB).

Here we find a portrayal of Christ found nowhere else in Scripture.[2] Revelation's Jesus is not the Gospels' man of sorrows, but King and Lord over the entire universe. He is not a weakened Christ doggedly tempted in the wilderness, thirsting at Jacob's well, or a tragic Christ nailed on the cross. Nor is He a benevolent Christ holding little children in His arms, a compassionate Christ touching a leper, or a Socratic Christ in sharp-edged dialogue with Nicodemus.[3] Rather we behold a majestic, commanding, glorious, powerful Christ. An eternal Christ who never changes. And a sovereign Christ who challenges us to follow Him today. He is a Christ that we can love.[4]

Think of the imagery here. Standing in the middle of seven golden lampstands, He wears glistening white robes and has white hair. Jesus has fiery eyes, molten red feet, and an arresting voice. His hands clutch stars, a sword emerges from His mouth, and His face shines like the sun. Jesus reveals Himself to John in the language of prophetic symbolism (drawn primarily from Daniel 7 and 10), not in a literal depiction of His resurrection body as He now sits at God's right hand. We are not to think that the glorified body in which Jesus ascended to heaven has a sword in place of a tongue, snow-white hair, or a face so overpowering with physical light that the pure in heart cannot view it with joy (see Matt. 5:8; Rev. 22:4). The symbols seen by John in the vision reveal not what Jesus looks like, but what He is like. They depict Him as the searcher of hearts, full of consuming holiness and boundless wisdom. He is the perfect priest standing for His people before the Father, the perfect king defending them against the devil by His invincible Word. Revelation's visions show us how things are, not how they might appear to the physical senses.[5] Such images let us feel and connect with who Jesus really is—thus providing all the hope and encouragement we could ask for.[6]

From this grand opening Revelation unveils a virtual gallery of pictures of Christ.[7] Jesus is one like a son of man (Rev. 1:13), the first and the last (verse 17), the lamb and the lion (Rev. 5:5, 6), the thief in the night (Rev. 3:3; 16:15), both priest and sacrifice (Rev. 1:5, 13; 5:6; 8:3, 4), the one who was dead and came to life (Rev. 1:18; 2:8), King of kings and Lord of lords (Rev. 17:14; 19:16), the divine judge riding a white horse (Rev. 19:11-21), and the heavenly bridegroom (verses 7-9). These and other metaphors tumble out of John's fertile mind. We see Jesus now supervising His churches (Rev. 1:9-3:21), now sharing God's throne in heaven (Rev. 4; 5), now controlling the course of history (Rev. 6:1-8:1), now calling the world to repentance (Rev. 8:3-11:19), now standing victoriously on Mount Zion with 144,000 faithful followers (Rev. 14:1-5), now riding a white horse in judgment (Rev. 19:11-21), now promising to return soon to claim and to marry His bride (Rev. 19:7-9; 22:7, 12, 20), and now beckoning and encouraging with His grace (Rev. 22:17, 21).

Such vivid images assure us that the connection between God and His people is close and definite. Jesus Christ is everything that we need, especially as history approaches its close.[8] Thus Scripture's last words on Christ leave us waiting, hoping, expecting, longing, clinging to the threefold promise that Jesus is coming soon (Rev. 22:7, 12, 20, 17). Revelation is all about Jesus and why we should love Him!

The Only Right Response

Notice what happens to John when He meets this eternal Christ—the Jesus he loves and whom he hasn't seen in more than 60-plus years. He makes the only right response that humans can when confronted by the eternal Christ. "When I saw Him, I fell at his feet like a dead man" (Rev. 1:17, NASB). The radiance and purity of the exalted Jesus overwhelm him. Conscious of his weakness and sinfulness before a holy and commanding Lord, he falls down at His feet like a dead person, just as he had done earlier on the Mount of Transfiguration (verse 17; cf. Matt. 17:6). Jesus is bigger than John, and the disciple can't handle it. No human being can. Daniel's reaction to a similar vision was the same:

"As soon as I heard the sound of his words, I fell into a deep sleep on my face, with my face to the ground. Then behold, a hand touched me and set me trembling on my hands and knees. . . . When he had spoken to me according to these words, I turned my face toward the ground and became speechless. . . . 'O my lord, as a result of the vision anguish has come upon me, and I have retained no strength'" (Dan. 10:9-16, NASB).

Isaiah's woeful sense of defilement in the presence of "the King, the Lord of hosts" (Isa. 6:5, NASB) and Paul's collapse to the roadway before Jesus' blinding light (Acts. 9:4) show the sheer shock that mere mortals experience when confronted by the Holy One. If the experience of biblical prophets is any measure, being slain by God's holy presence is anything but pleasant. Even holy angels cover their eyes in deference to God's glory (Isa. 6:1-5).

Here is more than sheer overpowering physical light that blinds the eye. It is a consuming holiness and glory that pierces moral consciousness.[9] Whenever God reveals Himself, or discloses something about Himself, it forces human beings to recognize something about themselves. His divine holiness invades their private world. It cannot be avoided. Insight into God's moral nature brings insight into their own. Ethical implications touch the conscience, highlighting character and throwing it into moral and spiritual contrast with God.

Revelation's imagery of Christ's eyes as flames of fire reveals Him as the one who searches the mind and heart (Rev. 1:14; 19:12, cf. 2:23). Nothing remains hidden from Christ's penetrating gaze. He sees everything there is to see (Ps. 139). His eyes don't look *at* us but right *into* us. His holiness gets inside us, and when it does, it challenges us. And if we allow, it will change us!

In his *Confessions* Augustine quips, "You set me in front of my own face."[10] "When I get into the presence of God," Oswald Chamber writes, "I do not realize that I am a sinner in an indefinite sense; I realize the concentration of sin in a particular feature of my life. A man will say easily—'Oh, yes, I know I am a sinner'; but when he gets into the presence of God he cannot get off with that statement. The conviction is concentrated on—I am this, or that, or the other. This is always the sign that a man or woman is in the presence of God. There is never any vague sense of sin, but the concentration of sin in some personal particular. God begins by convicting us of the one thing fixed on in the mind that is prompted by His Spirit; if we will yield to His conviction on that point, He will lead us down to the great disposition of sin underneath. That is the way God always deals with us when we are consciously in His presence."[11]

"The closer you come to Jesus," Ellen White observes, "the more faulty you will appear in your own eyes; for your vision will be clearer, and your imperfections will be seen in broad and distinct contrast to His perfect nature. This is evidence that Satan's delusions have lost their power; that the vivifying influence of the Spirit of God is arousing you. No deep-seated love for Jesus can dwell in the heart that does not realize its own sinfulness. The soul that is transformed by the grace of Christ will admire His divine character; but if we do not see our own moral deformity, it is unmistakable evidence that we have not had a view of the beauty and excellence of Christ."[12]

If such things can happen in a heart without the presence of visible physical phenomenon, we can only imagine what it would be like to see, as did John, the eternal Christ in person. But John is a microcosm of the church, a brother of his hearers who shares with them a threefold treasure: "the tribulation and kingdom and perseverance which are in Jesus" (Rev. 1:9, NASB).[13] His experience with Jesus is paradigmatic, suggesting that we too—through faith's eye—can share John's experience and behold the eternal Christ. Such is the power of Scripture and the mighty work of the Holy Spirit, who speaks in behalf of Christ (Rev. 2:7, 11, 17, 29; 3:6, 13, 22).

Revelation's opening vision reminds us that Jesus is always more than we anticipate, more than we bargained for, and infinitely more than we will ever be. In fact, He is more than some of us care to have around or to get too close to or even to look at (Rev. 6:16). Yet I hear John saying, "This is precisely why I love Jesus. I love Him because He is bigger than me. He does something to me deep down inside whenever I meet Him. I see myself as I really am—a weak, sinful person in great need and incapable in myself of ever being like Him. The eternal Jesus reads my thoughts and understands my heart. He recognizes the real me (which I often don't see myself)! Not only holding me accountable, He challenges me and He wants to change me. Christ's blazing eyes may be unnerving, but I welcome His piercing gaze. Not only do I want to know what He sees in me, but I need to know if there is anything in me that shouldn't be there (Ps. 139:24). Anything that dishonors either Him or me. I cannot see Jesus and remain the same. Above all, I want to see a Jesus who is and can do what I can never be or do. While I am inadequate and vulnerable, my eternal Christ is able and mighty!"

He Touched Me! /

While our hearts grapple with the moral implications of gazing into the blazing eyes and blinding face of Jesus, we must look ahead and see what this eternal Christ does when John falls at His feet like one slain. Jesus places His right hand on him, saying, "Do not be afraid; I am the first and the last, and the living One; and I was dead, and behold, I am alive forevermore, and I have the keys of death and of Hades" (Rev. 1:17, 18, NASB).

Imagine the scene. John lies prostrate on the ground, face buried in his hands. Jesus now touches him with His right hand. To do so, Jesus must bend down low. You cannot touch a man lying prostrate on the floor with your hand unless you do so! The glorious, majestic, intimidating, holy Jesus bends down to touch His servant John. I imagine Him almost kneeling, just as He did when He washed John's feet in the upper room (John 13:1-17).

Not only does Jesus touch John—He talks to him. The commanding voice that had thundered like a trumpet and rushing waters now speaks comfort—comfort based on Jesus' mighty power. They are words of hope and promise. "John, don't be afraid of Me. As the First and Last I have power over time. As the Living One, I have power over life. As the one who was dead and alive forever, I have power over sin. And because I have the keys of death and the grave, I have power over death."[14]

That touch tells us why John or anyone else would ever love Jesus. The gesture is personal and intimate. When you reach out to touch someone who is frightened or hurting, you do so because you care. Jesus

23

touches John because He cares. I hear an echo from Daniel 10, in which the glorious being whom Daniel saw touched him too, saying, "O Daniel, greatly loved of God, listen carefully to what I have to say to you" (Dan. 10:11, NLT). Not only does Jesus touch John, but He offers words of comfort. Jesus gets personal with him because he was the disciple that Jesus loved (John 13:23; 19:26; 20:2; 21:7, 20). The Apocalypse reveals this awesome, majestic, commanding (even intimidating) holy Jesus as personal. He's the same Jesus who touched people while on earth: the leper, the blind, the sick, and the trembling who could not handle holiness (Matt. 8:3, 15; 9:29; 17:7; 20:34). Scripture's last book reveals Jesus as both the eternal Christ who is bigger than we are, and as the Personal Christ who is never too big for me and you.

In his opening vision of Jesus, John experiences Him in three ways. He hears Him (Rev. 1:10), sees Him (verses 12, 17), and feels Him (verse 17). Hearing, seeing, and touching are one of the disciple's recurring themes. He writes about it in his First Epistle: "What was from the beginning, what we have heard, what we have seen with our eyes, what we have looked at and touched with our hands, concerning the Word of Life—and the life was manifested, and we have seen and testify and proclaim to you the eternal life, which was with the Father and was manifested to us—what we have seen and heard we proclaim to you also, so that you too may have fellowship with us; and indeed our fellowship is with the Father, and with His Son Jesus Christ. These things we write, so that our joy may be made complete" (1 John 1:1-4, NASB). I heard Jesus, saw Jesus, and touched Him. So can you, John implies.

In his Gospel John likewise saw, heard, and touched Jesus. Now, on the rocky island of Patmos, 60-plus years later, he hears and sees and feels His eternal Christ once more. The reality that the book of Revelation points to here is not that of physical appearance, or audible voice, or tangible touch, but the personal nature of Jesus' connection with those whom He loves. Again, Revelation's vision of Jesus shows us how things are, not how they look to the physical eye.[15] They let us feel and connect with who Jesus really is, thus providing all the hope and encouragement we could ask for.[16]

What John experiences with Jesus is representative of the church as a whole. We may never see the glorious face or hear the audible voice or feel the physical touch of Christ until He appears in the clouds, but we can be sure that the Jesus of Revelation is not an elusive, impersonal, and unapproachable being. His face and voice and touch are just as real now as He was then. We can behold His face (2 Cor. 3:18; 4:6; Heb. 2:9; 12:2), hear His voice (Heb. 2:7; John 10:27; Heb. 3:15), and experience His touch through His Word, Spirit, and holy presence in our lives. Revelation proclaims that Jesus Christ is everything that we need, especially as history rushes to its close.[17] Again, its vivid personal images assure us that the connection between God and His people is close and definite.

Loving the Unseen Christ

Thus Scripture's last word reveals Jesus as both the eternal Christ who is bigger than me, and the personal Christ who is never too big for me. We behold a majestic, commanding, glorious, powerful, and holy Christ whose presence and gaze pierces moral consciousness and will ever unsettle us. Yet that Jesus is personal. He reaches out to us in an intimate way with comfort, hope, purpose, and help.

As I read these things I wonder: Do I see the eternal Christ? Or is He too much like me? Do I have a keen sense of just how great He really is—holy, majestic, commanding, King of kings and Lord of lords? Am I in awe of Him? Have I gotten close enough to Him to realize just how sinful I really am, or am I so familiar (too close and casual) with Him that I've lost touch with who He really is (and who I am as well)? Do I really believe that Jesus is big enough to meet the needs of my life and the world I face each day?

On the other hand, do I see the personal Christ? Or is He too big, too far away, too transcendent and detached to care for me? Do I relate to Jesus personally? Do I see Him as a personal Lord who cares, loves, and relates with me?

Our imaginations are constricted. We see Jesus walking around Palestine with a bunch of dense fishermen, helping people, holding babies, saying things suitable for memorizing in church or placing on a decorative plaque, and dying on the cross—and we suppose we have it all. Like Christo Javacheff's *Wrapped Reichstag,* John's Revelation of Jesus Christ trains us to resee Jesus in whatever terms are necessary to affirm Him as first and last and center. The visions make our imaginations supple and alert, so that we may realize that Jesus provides the grounding for our lives no matter what the situation.[18]

The Revelation of Jesus Christ is not just vision. Bringing self-awareness, it forges trust ("Fear not; I am . . .") and initiates a task for John.[19] "Write what you see," Jesus commands. Thus the aged disciple has work to do.

REVELATION'S GREAT LOVE STORY

Prior to the vision John is on the prison island in isolated exile, cut off from his churches. Rome is the ascendant power. From a human point of view, the gospel appears weak and ineffective against unstoppable evil. Everything John believed and preached is, to all evidence, a disaster. And then suddenly he sees Jesus again, anew. Set on his feet, he has a message and a job. John exiled is now John empowered. No wonder that he loves Jesus! The vision—the revelation of Jesus Christ—did it. Visions, if they are truly visions and not dreams of wish fulfillment, make things happen.[20]

The vision of Jesus in Revelation can make things happen with every one of us as well. It can lead us to view Him in a way that will cause us never to be the same again. So much so that we will love Jesus with all our heart.

I likely will never have a vision of Jesus as John did, nor touch Him personally, nor audibly hear His voice, but the disciple's experience gives me the assurance that I can be filled with the wonder of Jesus and that He will relate to me personally. I can love the unseen Christ! "You love him even though you have never seen him," Peter writes, and "though you do not see him, you trust him; and even now you are happy with a glorious, inexpressible joy" (1 Peter 1:8, NLT). That's what I want, and it's what Revelation opens before me.

And so I wonder what I need to do to relate to Jesus as the Eternal. To stand in awe and wonder before Him with reverence, confession, and self-surrender. And what do I do to relate to Jesus personally? To think about Him and commune with Him and listen carefully to what He has to say? How should I search for where He is at work in my life and world? Immersing myself in Scripture's last word on Jesus Christ must surely be part of it.

[1] Paul Goldberger, "Christo's Wrapped Reichstag: Symbol of the New Germany," *New York Times,* June 23, 1995.

[2] Ranko Stefanovic, *Revelation of Jesus Christ: Commentary on the Book of Revelation* (Berrien Springs, Mich.: Andrews University Press, 2002), p. 56.

[3] Eugene H. Peterson, *Reversed Thunder: The Revelation of John and the Praying Imagination* (San Francisco: Harper and Row, 1991), p. 29.

[4] John Stott, *The Incomparable Christ* (Downers Grove, Ill.: InterVarsity Press, 2001), p. 233.

[5] Dennis E. Johnson, *The Triumph of the Lamb: A Commentary on Revelation* (Phillipsburg, N. J.: P & R Publishing, 2001), p. 60.

[6] Kendell H. Easley, *Revelation* (Nashville: Broadman and Holman, 1998), p. 23.

[7] Stott, *The Incomparable Christ,* p. 169.

[8] Stefanovic, p. 64.

[9] John N. Oswalt, *The Book of Isaiah: Chapters 1-39* (Grand Rapids: William B.

Eerdmans, 1986), p. 181.

[10] Augustine, *Confessions,* VIII, p. 124.

[11] Oswald Chambers, "The Concentration of Personal Sin," *My Utmost for His Highest,* July 3.

[12] Ellen G. White, *Steps to Christ,* pp. 64, 65.

[13] Johnson, p. 55.

[14] Easley, p. 20.

[15] Johnson, p. 60.

[16] Easley, p. 23.

[17] Stefanovic, p. 64.

[18] Peterson, pp. 39, 40.

[19] *Ibid.,* p. 40.

[20] *Ibid.,* p. 41.

HE CANCELS MY DEBTS

Look Again . . . for the First Time
Revelation 1:4-6

I lay in bed on a Friday night at our school in Sagunto, Spain, wondering out loud to God why I was there. Eager to get home and see my family, I hadn't really wanted this final leg of my almost three-week-long trip through Poland, Portugal, and Spain. That next morning I met Peter Colquhoun, a retired church leader from Australia. Since neither of us knew any Spanish and no one offered to translate for us, finding each other was an immediate mutual blessing. Once we got to talking, we became oblivious to everything around us.

During our time together, Peter shared how he and his wife, Carelle, made a covenant that when they retired they would turn their energies toward volunteer mission service. That was why they were in Sagunto—to teach English to our seminary students there. Before Sagunto, however, they spent 15 months in Thailand at an English language program teaching English to Thai professionals, university teachers, and university students. Carelle, who has a master's degree in teaching English as a second language, would have the language students first. With her they would learn the basics. Then they migrated to Peter, who practiced English with them, helping them develop a wider vocabulary and understanding of the language. At this phase of their learning, Peter purposely integrated the Bible into their reading. He focused their attention on key biblical words and concepts to help them understand what they were reading—common words to you and me, such as "faith," "justification," "obedience," "commandments," "sin," "forgiveness," "death," "judgment," "salvation," and "substitution." His goal was to enable these Buddhists, Muslims, or secular individuals to grasp what the words meant and how to use them in conversation, reading, or writing. In the process he sought to unfold the biblical worldview and lay a foundation for sharing the gospel.

One day Peter announced, "I want to tell you a story." He then proceeded to take the entire class period to relate the biblical account of Jesus and His death for them—about God's love and the plan of salvation. Now, no one in the class had ever heard the gospel before. At least not with any understanding. While Peter shared the narrative of the cross, a hush fell over the classroom. "It was as if they were transfixed. Awed," he told me, tears forming in his eyes, lips quivering. His voice filled with emotion. It deeply moved him just to relive it. His account riveted me, and tears formed in my own eyes as I listened.

"When the bell rang for class to end," he continued, "no one moved. Rather than rushing out as usual, they just sat there, looking at me. So I took my time and finished the story. Then I invited them to give their hearts to Jesus. And I asked them to bow their heads while I prayed for them. I hadn't done that before—prayed with them. But this time I did. I prayed for them to understand what they had just heard about Jesus and His death for them. To believe and receive Jesus. When I finished, they still just sat there. It seemed as if no one wanted to leave. Then, one by one, they quietly got up and walked out."

With tears still brimming, Peter told of baptizing scores of such students during the 15 months he and Carelle were in Thailand. Choked up at what I had heard, I praised God out loud. This is why we're here—to tell of Jesus' death. To proclaim the gospel.

At that moment I thought about Revelation's slain Lamb and why I love Jesus. Here were people hearing about the substitutionary death of Jesus Christ on their behalf for the very first time. Transfixed and visibly moved, they found themselves under deep conviction to do something about it. It was a thrilling moment of insight, conviction, desire, and decision.

Most of my readers, though, have heard the story of Jesus, the "good news" of the gospel, so many times that it's not so new (and gripping) anymore. Constantly singing and talking about it, we assume that we understand it. When I think of those Thai English language students, transfixed at their first hearing of the story of Jesus and its implications for their own lives, I wonder how most of us still respond to this same story. Is it possible that it's become too familiar? that maybe we've missed its meaning or that its significance has lost its grip on us? Or perhaps that we really don't have a clear understanding of such things as sin, forgiveness, or justification? While we know vocabulary—the lingo—we haven't grasped it by experience. So the blood of Jesus, the sacrifice of Jesus, doesn't touch us the same way anymore or even at all. Although we might sing about loving Jesus, our lives portray something entirely different. I see the same thing taking place in the church today that John did at the end of the first century—its love for Jesus was growing cold (Rev. 2:4; cf. 3:15). Jesus said that it will again happen in the end as the love of many fades until they can no longer hold on and endure (Matt. 24:12, 13). Revelation correctly links such waning love to a loss of perspective concerning the blood of Jesus—His substitutionary death.

And so I read John—who was there when Jesus died and who saw the blood flowing from His side (John 19:34-37)—telling us again something very important about Jesus: "To Him who loves us and released us from our sins by His blood. . . . To Him be the glory and the dominion forever and ever. Amen!" (Rev. 1:5, 6, NASB). Just to talk about Jesus and His love gets the old disciple excited. Unable to stop himself from singing this first hymn of the Apocalypse, he wants to give Jesus glory and dominion over his life. "I love Jesus," John says. "I love Him because He cancels my debts and and releases me from my sins by His blood." The passage pairs the verb "loves" with the next verb "released" in such a way that the first may be seen as the basis for the second.[1] John has no doubt in his mind that Christ expressed His love by redeeming His people from their sins through His *death* ("blood").[2] Jesus specifically and powerfully demonstrated His love in His atoning "blood" that has "freed us from our sins" (verse 5, NIV).

Somehow I sense that if I am to love Jesus (like John, ever breaking into doxological praise of Him when I think of His love and how He demonstrated it) then I need to see these things again and again—and each new time as if it were the first time. I will love Jesus in proportion to my sense of canceled debts. "I tell you," Jesus told Simon the night he criticized Mary for anointing His feet with costly perfume, "her sins—and they are many—have been forgiven, so she has shown me much love. But a person who is forgiven little shows only little love" (Luke 7:47, NLT).

Forever Forsaken

In order to experience the full meaning of this awesome truth that John writes about here at the beginning of the Apocalypse, we need to fast-forward to near the end of Revelation's gripping story. In Revelation 20 we encounter one of the most sobering and chilling Bible truths—the "second death" (Rev. 20:6, 14; cf. 21:8; 2:11). The book of Revelation reminds us that there exist two kinds of death, and where it speaks of a "second death" it uses some of the most horrifying words in all human language. Revelation 20 opens to our understanding the serious reality of the "second death." It is more than a physical death of the body. In fact, the physical death by literal fire would seem to be a kind of sweet release from the soul anguish inherent in the second death.

Let's imagine that the 1,000 years of Revelation 20 has ended. Released from his prison, Satan whips up the resurrected lost to attack the people of God in one last battle. As the wicked surround the New Jerusalem, John says, "Fire came down from God out of heaven and devoured them" (Rev. 20:9, NKJV). The book of Revelation makes it clear that the lake of fire is the "second death" reserved for those who reject both the Lamb and the ethics of the new heaven and earth (verse 14; 21:8). However, the fire from heaven is not the whole picture of the second death. So John backs up to give a more detailed description of what will take place before fire devours the wicked. The literal fire that consumes flesh and bone is the lesser part of the second death. It is, in fact, its merciful conclusion.

Notice how John goes on to describe the second death: "Then I saw a great white throne and Him who sat upon it, from whose presence earth and heaven fled away, and no place was found for them. And I saw the dead, the great and the small, standing before the throne, and books were opened; and another book was opened, which is the book of life; and the dead were judged from the things which were written in the books, according to their deeds. And the sea gave up the dead which were in it, and death and Hades gave up the dead which were in them; and they were judged, every one of them according to their deeds. Then death and Hades were thrown into the lake of fire. This is the second death, the lake of fire. And if anyone's name was not found written in the book of life, he was thrown into the lake of fire" (Rev. 20:11-15, NASB).

The second death is initiated by a full revelation of God seated upon "a great white throne" with His "face" fully exposed to the astonished gaze of all (the Greek word *pro,swpon*, translated "presence," means "face, countenance, appearance"). We meet here a full, unveiled encounter with God. In Revelation everyone ultimately will behold God's unveiled face (Rev. 6:16, 17; 20:11, 12; 22:4). All will stand before His throne and see His face. But all will not think the same thoughts and experience the same feelings as they meet the undimmed reality of God's character.[3] Everyone will be conscious of themselves in relation to His holiness. Earlier in Revelation we read how the lost will find themselves compelled to flee away from Jesus when He returns (Rev. 6:15-17). They will feel an irrepressible impulse to run and hide. The divine presence is unbearable because they have formed within themselves a character totally contrary to the holy God of love. We have seen already how even prophets and disciples have a hard time in the presence of the holy (cf. Rev. 1:17). Face and conscience are incredible moral realities in Revelation.

Here as God appears on His great white throne, we again find ourselves confronted with that awesome reality of face and conscience as even a personified heaven and earth flee in fear of divine judgment. That little sentence at the end of Revelation 20:11—"There was no place found for them" (NKJV)—are some of the most horrifying words in all human language (Rev. 12:8; Dan. 2:35). If there is no place for heaven and earth, what of sinners? Not only will they cringe in light of God's unveiled presence, they will experience a terrifying sense of separation from God and utter aloneness. "There's no place for me here!" they will tell themselves. Overwhelmed with a deep inner sense of complete unbelonging, the wicked standing before God's throne realize with intense vividness that they are so out of harmony with the universe that it has absolutely no place for them.[4] Because they don't fit, they cannot exist in the coming new moral spiritual order. And from the depths of their horrified souls they will cry out, "No, God, don't forsake me! Don't leave me alone. Please. Noooooooooooo!"

Then the books are opened (Rev. 20:12). Everyone now standing before the throne is judged according to what's found in them—their works. In this unfolding drama of unveiled encounter with God the second death brings the lost face to face with the full, ugly reality of their sin. It is an awareness that can no longer be tempered by divine mercy.[5] Unable anymore to ignore what they have become, they will have a deep consciousness of the sin that they have committed. Sin exists as an undeniable reality in their mind. Not only is it written down in the heavenly books—it is on record in their conscience. The horror of the moment is both objective and existential.

In order to grasp what Revelation pictures here, try to imagine what it would be like if you were made perfectly conscious of every sin you ever committed—every wrong thought and feeling and action. Acutely aware of every ugly detail, you realize that you no longer have any way of escaping their consequences. Then add to that horrendous picture an absolute absence of mercy—no possibility of forgiveness or acceptance. No picture of God who freely and eagerly pardons all sin. What would that kind of moment in time be like for you?[6]

In his book *The Sunflower* Simon Wiesenthal wonders about the possibilities and limits of forgiveness. While imprisoned in a Nazi concentration camp, Simon one day found himself taken from his work detail to the bedside of a dying member of the SS. A young man named Karl lay there, his face covered with gray-yellow stained bandages with openings only for mouth, nose, and ears. "I have not much longer to live," he whispered in a weak, broken voice. "I know the end is near and am resigned to dying soon. But before that I want to talk about an experience that is torturing me. Otherwise I cannot die in peace."

Haunted by the crimes in which he had participated, he wanted to confess to and obtain forgiveness from a Jew. One event especially filled him with guilt and horror. It had happened on a hot summer day on the Russian front in Dnepropetrovsk when he and others received orders to round up nearly 200 Jews from the ravaged city and pack them like sardines into a house filled with cans full of gasoline. The house was not very large and had only three stories. It seemed impossible to cram so many people into it. But after a few minutes not a Jew remained on the street. Then another truck arrived full of more Jews, and the SS troops crammed them into the building with the others. The Germans locked the door and mounted machine guns to prevent any escape. Then came the command to remove the safety pins from hand grenades and hurl them through the windows of the house. Detonations followed. The screams were horrible. Flames ate their way from floor to floor. Dense smoke poured out and choked the troops guarding the inferno. Karl and others had their rifles ready to shoot anyone who tried to escape from the blazing hell.

Behind the windows of the second floor a man held a small child in his arms. His clothes were aflame. By his side stood a woman, doubtless his wife. As Karl watched, with his free hand the man covered the child's eyes . . . then he jumped through the window into the street. Seconds later the mother followed. Then from the other windows fell burning bodies. "We shot," Karl groaned. "Oh, God! I don't know how many tried to leap out of the windows, but that one family I shall never forget—least of all the child. It had black hair and dark eyes. . . . I see then plainly before my eyes . . . I am left here in my guilt. In the last hours of my life you are with me. I do not know who you are. I only know that you are a Jew and that is enough.

REVELATION'S GREAT LOVE STORY

"I want to die in peace, and so I need forgiveness . . . from a Jew."

I Here lay a man in bed who wished to die in peace, but could not, because the memory of his terrible crime gave him no rest. Faced with the choice between compassion and justice, silence and truth, Wiesenthal said nothing. He just turned around and walked out of the room, leaving Karl to die with the horror of a guilt-haunted heart—separated from both God and self.[7]

Thus Revelation pictures the lost gathered around God's throne, judged by the books that chronicle every sin they have ever committed. By some divinely chosen method every hardened rebel will see the part he or she has played in the great war between good and evil. Every deed of their lives will be etched with vivid clarity upon their mind's eye. The blazing light of infinite love will clash in their souls with the dark ugliness of sin.[8]

The reality is that human beings don't have to wait till that horrifying moment at the end of the millennium to be haunted with the reality of sin, guilt, shame, and unbelonging—separation from God. Remember how Americans were surprised when Katherine Ann Power suddenly reappeared in 1993 and surrendered herself to the FBI after 23 years on the run. The tragic 1970 Boston bank heist, in which police officer William Schroeder was mercilessly submachined-gunned in the back, sent Power on a long odyssey of internal turmoil. Through the years she became Alice Metzinger, someone with a new identity and a whole new life.

To some, Kathy Power had become something of a mythic figure. Always out there, always free. The one that the police couldn't catch. But she finally was caught. Not by the FBI, but by herself—by her conscience. Inside she had the haunting memory of a crime that would not let go of her thoughts. Struggling with her secrets, she became so emotionally and psychologically worn down that she could no longer go on. She had to do something about it. After months of intense therapy she finally decided to come clean. Power's husband told *Time* magazine that "she wanted her life back. She wanted her truth back. She wants to be whole." Katherine herself said, "I know that I must answer this accusation from the past, in order to live with full authenticity in the present."[9]

If we are harboring some sin—if we are keeping hidden a few secret regions of wrong—we can't expect to enjoy freedom from guilt. Scipture has an unspoken axiom threaded throughout it: secret sin cannot coexist with inner peace. Peace returns only when we fully confess and forsake our sins. Nothing is more grinding than an unforgiven conscience.[10]

Have you ever felt sinful and unclean as your habits, mind, feelings, and inner self gravitate toward things that you know are wrong? And you can't get rid of thoughts or feelings about your actions or ways or who you really are? Such experiences and deeds leave you feeling distant from God and the church. Although you yearn to go in a different direction you feel totally powerless to do so. After all, you've already failed so many times. Your past haunts you every moment of your life. The fact is that we don't have to wait till the end of the 1,000 years to experience the reality of the second death. We can feel alone and separated from God even now.

The Passion of Jesus

Let's consider for a moment the "blood" of Jesus—His death (Rev. 1:5). What death did Jesus die? Be careful now! Yes, He died a physical death. It was real blood splattered all over the place of His beating and crucifixion (blood made all too vivid in Mel Gibson's *Passion of the Christ*). John saw the physical blood and death of Jesus and graphically told about it in his Gospel (John 18; 19). We can be sure that Revelation's reference to Jesus' blood is not metaphorical! Yet it draws us beyond the physical death of Jesus toward that "second death" experience that Revelation so vividly unfolds.

Remember what Jesus said about Himself when He entered Gethsemane? "My soul [not His body] is crushed with grief to the point of death" (Matt. 26:38, NLT). "My soul is overwhelmed with sorrow to the point of death" (verse 38, NIV). Jesus was already dying when He entered Gethsemane. He said that its cause was a grief so intense that it was lethal. Jesus was not dying because of physical reasons. He was experiencing a soul-level death. Something that exceeds sorrow was preying on His inner person.[11] Jesus was entering the dark realm of the second death—the death that involves the soul.

Isaiah 53 foretold how the Christ would suffer and die at the soul level of being.[12] Three times it asserted that His suffering and death would center in His "soul" (Hebrew, *nephesh*, i.e., soul, self, life): "You make His soul an offering for sin. . . . He shall see the labor of His soul. . . . He poured out His soul unto death" (Isa. 53:10-12, NKJV). His sufferings would be "soul suffering." Notice that the prophet makes little if any mention of physical suffering. Rather it describes a deeper agony that occurs on the internal, emotional level. It portrays soul sorrow and grief and agony and sin and condemnation and guilt (see Isa. 53:3-5, 7, 8, 10-12).

REVELATION'S GREAT LOVE STORY

The heart and mind of Jesus was plunged into the collective whole of all human evil as though He were the only guilty party. Taking it into Himself, He experienced the full brunt of the mental and emotional horror that sin's condemnation ultimately imposes on the inner consciousness of the soul.[13] That's why we hear Him asking His Father in Gethsemane, "If it is possible, let this cup of suffering be taken away from me" (Matt. 26:39, NLT). Already, there in Gethsemene, Jesus drank Revelation's "wine of the wrath of God, which is poured out without mixture" (Rev. 14:10). The dreaded cup symbolized neither the physical pain of being flogged and crucified, nor the mental distress of being despised and rejected even by His own people, but rather the spiritual agony of bearing the sins of the world, i.e., enduring the divine judgment those sins deserved.[14] Thus Jesus enters fully into the bridgeless chasm that exists between God's holy love and human self-absorbed sinfulness. By venturing into the mental and emotional suffering inherent in wrongdoing, something no human being has ever had to face on their own account because of the shielding mercy of God,[15] He found His soul filled with the incomprehensible dread of separation from God. In His agony He clung to the cold ground as if to prevent Himself from drifting further from God.[16]

Consider also the shuddering cry from the cross: "My God, my God, why have you forsaken me?" (Matt. 27:46, NIV). Here is the real sacrifice, the true suffering, the death that He shrank from in Gethsemane. In fact, the agony He endured in Gethsemane opens a window on the greater agony He went through on the cross. If just to anticipate the bearing of human sin and divine wrath was so terrible, what must the reality have been like?[17] Hanging there between heaven and earth, Jesus feels the separation that sin will ultimately open up between God and unrepentant sinners. The three-hour darkness that enveloped the cross was an outward symbol of the spiritual darkness that surrounded His soul (verses 45, 46). For what is darkness in biblical symbolism but separation from God, who is light and in whom "there is no darkness at all" (1 John 1:5, NIV)? In fact, Jesus used "outer darkness" as one of His expressions for hell, since it involves an absolute exclusion from the light of the divine presence. Our sins condemned the Son of God to that same outer darkness.[18]

In the darkness Jesus felt absolutely alone. God-forsaken, He suffered in His soul the terrible torment of a condemned and abandoned sinner. He alone has borne it. Not one person in all of history has yet experienced the full wages of sin. Thus, when the darkness was absolute, with no life beyond the grave in sight, Jesus chose our eternal life over His own.

Released!

One of the places I visited while in Portugal was the Museum of Sacred Art in Braga (a short distance north of Porto). It's just a small museum, but it has a collection of precious works of sacred art from the sixteenth to eighteenth centuries. On display are elaborately carved ivory crucifixes (including the largest in the world, in which you can even see the tongue and teeth of Jesus, whose mouth is twisted by pain). The museum also has embroidered vestments that weigh up to 40 pounds or more, a fourteenth-century statue of the virgin Mary, and a Gothic chalice from the same period, as well as silver and gilt monstrances adorned with diamonds.

What I was most interested in was a plain metal cross used at the celebration of the first Mass in Brazil, following the country's discovery by Portugal's Pedro Álvares Cabral in 1500. As I viewed that simple metal object (maybe 11 inches for the post and 8 inches at the crossbeam) through two layers of thick glass, I heard our tour guide say that it was worth $150 million. *$150 million?* I thought to myself. I had already noted some obvious exaggeration and biased misinformation on the part of our guide. The sheer volume of sacred lore he presented made me question the truth of some of it. So I wondered if a plain metal cross with hardly anything etched on it could really be worth that much. Maybe. Maybe not. But even if it were, who would want it? Not me!

But when it comes to the real cross and the death of Jesus, one estimates its value against Revelation's second death and the fact that Jesus frees us from that horrifying experience.

John tells us that Jesus "loves us and released us from our sins by His blood" (Rev. 1:5, NASB). The Greek word for "released" is the first one every seminary student learns when they study Greek—*lu,w* (*luo*). It means "to loose, untie, release, set free something that or someone who has been bound, chained, imprisoned, tied up." Here John uses it as a metaphor in the sense of setting us free from the brute power of sin to hold us in its thrall. The imagery implies that individuals are held captive by their sins and that Christ's death has secured release from death's authority.[19] Thus John connects the blood/death of Jesus directly with the severing of the hold that our sins have over us.[20] It liberates us from our bondage to the penalty and power of sin by identifying through faith with Jesus' sacrificial death.

We find here associations with the Exodus Passover, in which God rescued Israel from slavery in Egypt.[21] In his Gospel John portrays Jesus as saying to His antagonists, "I tell you the truth, everyone who sins is a slave to sin" (John 8:34, NIV). We know the idea also from Romans 6:16-23, which speaks of being enslaved to sin; from Titus 2:14, which mentions redemption from iniquity; and from 1 Peter 1:18, 19, which describes redemption from the futile ways inherited from pagan forebears. Each passage uses the image of sin as slavery or as a slaveholder from which the sinner must be freed, and all find the basis for that liberation in the death of Jesus.

In the imagery of John's Revelation, however, the horrible effects of sin are more than bondage or captivity. They combine aspects of an incalculable debt, a condition of defilement, and the burden of legal guilt.[22] "You were slain, and with your blood you purchased men for God," we hear the four living creatures and 24 elders sing (Rev. 5:9, NIV; cf. Rev. 14:3). The Lamb's blood (death) "bought" people for God out of every tribe and tongue and people and nation! Sin incurs a debt against God's holiness and justice, which has resulted in our being sold into slavery or captivity. Our debt and bondage to sin leads ultimately to death (Rom. 6:20-23). But nothing arbitrarily cancels the debt. Instead, the Lamb bought us out of captivity, thus paying the debt that had bound us over to sin and death. He did it with the price of His precious blood (1 Peter 1:18, 19).

In Revelation 7 John sees a vision of this very multitude of purchased people, a group "that no one could count, from every nation, tribe, people and language, standing before the throne and in front of the Lamb. They were wearing white robes and were holding palm branches in their hands" (verse 9, NIV). Later the book describes these saints clothed in white as those who have "come out of the great tribulation; they have washed their robes and made them white in the blood of the Lamb" (verse 14, NIV). Here we meet a paradox—blood that whitens. The redeemed wash their robes white in the Lamb's blood. Now we are dealing with the idea of sin not as a debt or bondage, but as defilement, rendering sinners impure and unfit for the presence of a holy God. The clothing metaphor (here "robes") represents the character as reflected in thought, values, and deeds. It is who we are in our inner private world, and all that we do because of what we are. The book of Revelation stresses how sin defiles and overwhelms us with the sense that we are impure and unfit for God's presence. We feel shame and guilt. And our conscience accuses us. John expresses this truth of sin as defilement elsewhere when he writes: "If we walk in the Light as He Himself is in the Light, we have fellowship with one another, and the blood of Jesus His Son cleanses us from all sin" (1 John 1:7, NASB). In light of Christ's love and sacrifice, we are to remind ourselves, "How much more . . . will the blood of Christ, who through the eternal Spirit offered himself unblemished to God, cleanse our consciences from acts that lead to death, so that we may serve the living God!" (Heb. 9:14, NIV; cf. Rev. 7:14, 15).

Revelation's imagery of sin incurring legal guilt focuses on accusation and condemnation. In Revelation 12 John sees a vision in which the great red dragon (Satan) is defeated explicitly in his role as *accuser* (verses 7-10). Each of the dragon's names, the "Devil" and "Satan" (verse 9), has the connotation of accuser or adversary. Accusations have to do with guilt, and thus we find ourselves confronted with the idea of sin as legal transgression.[23] In verse 11 the accuser, the one who would bring a charge against God's people, is decisively defeated. His claims in God's court have been stricken down through the blood of the Lamb. Christ's death has justifying power on behalf of the sinner. The language of the law court and legal guilt appears further in Revelation's prevailing judgment theme that opens record books and ultimately holds everyone accountable as it judges them by the things written therein (Rev. 14:7; 20:11-15; cf. 22:11, 12; 17:1-18:24; 19:1, 2).

The last verse of Revelation 20 tells us that "if anyone's name was not found written in the book of life, he was thrown into the lake of fire" (verse 15, NASB). Only for those whose names are in "the book of life" will the last judgment mean joyful vindication rather than shameful destruction. We can only wonder, *How can the mere appearance of one's name in "the book of life" counterbalance the damning evidence contained in the book of our deeds (Rev. 20:12)?*[24] It is because the "book of life" belongs to the Lamb who has been slain in sacrifice for those listed in it. (Rev. 13:8). John later refers to it as the "Lamb's book of life" (Rev. 21:27) and links it also with the cross (Rev. 13:8).[25] It is important to note that it is the *Lamb's book of life!* The imagery assumes substitutionary atonement and mediation. Ultimately, it is the blood of Jesus that releases a person from this epochal judgment. Although defiled, condemned, indebted, and sold into slavery, those whose names are written in the Lamb's book of life have, by His blood, been purchased for God and installed by Christ as pure and holy, acquitted priests in His kingdom (Rev. 20:2-6; 5:9, 10; 1:5, 6). Cleansed from sin, they have been freed of shame, guilt, and condemnation. They have become the Lamb's spotless bride (Rev. 19:7, 8).

Thus being "released from our sins by His blood" at Revelation's opening (1:5, NASB) ultimately brings us to the reality of the "second death" at its closing (21:8). The horrible effects of sin as brute bondage, incalculable debt, shameful defilement, and accusing legal guilt all converge here in a soul-wrenching horror of darkness, dereliction, despair, and death from which there is absolutely no escape, no resurrection. But the blood of Jesus releases the redeemed from it all!

Washing My Robes

When I think of the sense of forsakenness that Christ felt in both Gethsemane and on the cross I gain a sense of what it means to be released from my sins. Even when faced with the terrifying possibility of an eternal God-forsaken death, and knowing that He could abandon fallen humanity and save Himself at any moment, Jesus continued to trudge forward into the darkness with self-forgetful determination. At the cross of Christ we stand as breathless spectators witnessing the self-forgetful majesty of a love beyond our comprehension. "This is love: not that we loved God, but that he loved us and sent his Son as an atoning sacrifice for our sins" (1 John 4:10, NIV). "Jesus loves us," John assures. He "released us from our sins by His blood" (Rev. 1:5, NASB).

My heart stirs and surges with awe as the true significance of the Savior's sacrifice dawns within me. How could Jesus love me so deeply, so passionately, so selfishly? I've not seen the death of Jesus as John did. Nor can I imagine it as vividly as I would like. And I can scarcely grasp the existential horror of the "second death" of which he writes. But I know what shame and guilt are all about, just as John did. I have experienced the power of sin—its grip and hold. I have shared the burden of guilt and the sense of being unclean deep down inside. And I have felt the restless haunting of things that I've said or done or felt and seem never to be able to do or become. Sin is an existing reality in my mind and heart. It is on record in my conscience.

But I know, too, what it means to have my conscience cleansed from acts that lead to death and then to be empowered to serve the living God (Heb. 9:14). Because of Christ I have been forgiven and cleansed from all sin (1 John 1:9), and even though I may again sin, I have an advocate for me, Jesus Christ (1 John 2:1). Thus I can look with assurance, peace, and certainty to a future in which the "second death" has no power over me (Rev. 2:11; 20:6). I would, like John, likely fall down like a dead man in the presence of the eternal Christ, but I am confident that Jesus would tell me not to be afraid, that I can stand even at His appearing, because His grace is sufficient for me (Rev. 7:1-14).[26] Often I glance back to my teenage years when Jesus first released me from my sins! Tracing my life since then, I find myself overwhelmed with His love and never want His grace to have come to me in vain (1 Cor. 15:10). Instead, I ever want His gracious love to compel me to live my life passionately for Him (2 Cor. 5:14, 15).

Somehow I sense that if I am to love Jesus (like John, ever breaking into doxological praise of Him when I think of His love and how He demonstrated it) then I need to review these things again and again—and each new time as if it were the first time. I will love Jesus in proportion to my sense of canceled debts. "I tell you," Jesus told Simon the night he criticized Mary for anointing His feet with a year's supply of expensive perfume, "her sins— and they are many—have been forgiven, so she has shown me much love. But a person who is forgiven little shows only little love" (Luke 7:47, NLT). Just to talk about Jesus and His love gets John excited. He can't help singing Revelation's first hymn (Rev. 1:5, 6). John wants to give Jesus glory and dominion over his life. "I love Jesus," he says. "I love Him because He cancels my debts." That's why I love Jesus, too. He cancels my debts. As with the redeemed pictured before His throne, I would have my praise as everlasting as my redemption (Rev. 7:9, 10).

The doxological character of Revelation's presentation of Christ's atoning work, and the gratitude that it can inspire in the redeemed, gives us a glimpse into the nature and heart of the book (Rev. 1:5, 6; 5:9-12; 7:9, 10). Ellen White presses us ever to carefully read the prophecies of Revelation (and Daniel) in connection with the words, "Behold the Lamb of God, which taketh away the sin of the world" (1 John 1:29).[27]

Revelation tells of a moment when those who worship the beast and His image or receive a mark on their forehead or on their hand "will drink of the wine of the wrath of God, which is mixed in full strength in the cup of His anger; and he will be tormented with fire and brimstone in the presence of the holy angels and in the presence of the Lamb" (Rev. 14:10). I've often wondered what this imagery means. Why should moral beings receive judgment and be tormented in full view of other moral beings— holy angels and the Lamb? Is this right or just? Is this how a loving God does it? Will these holy angels and the Lamb take some kind of ghoulish delight on that dreadful day? Is it something they are looking forward to seeing or for some reason "must" see?

I wonder whether it is the fire and brimstone or the presence of holy angels and the Lamb that will cause the torment in the final phase of the judgment. Could it be the sense of love scorned (grace turned down) that hurts most? Perhaps it is the soul-shocking reality that they have ignored every

41

warning, every invitation, every opportunity, every provision to be saved, but chose otherwise, kept putting it off, or just didn't get around to knowing about Jesus and all He did for them. Think of the horror of dying in the presence of holy angels who did everything possible to help them come to the Lamb (Heb. 2:14). Of perishing in the presence of the Lamb slain in their behalf and whose own soul will cry out in unconsolable abandonment because of their decision. Could anything possibly be more overwhelming? Even as they drink the bitter dregs of final judgment and die the second death the Lamb is there to tell them that it is not what He wanted. "I have loved you with an everlasting love and have drawn you with lovingkindness," He explains, but you have been "unwilling to come to me so that you may have life" (John 5:40, NASB; cf. Jer. 31:3). "You didn't come to Me." Even as they perish they do so with the full knowledge that the blood of a slain Lamb could have released them from this very moment. Nothing will be more horrifying to lost souls than to know that they didn't need to die. That the very source of life is even now before them, but that it is too late.

The gospel is never about somebody else—it's always about you and me. It's always about actual persons, actual pain, actual trouble, actual sin: you; me; who you are and what you've done; who I am and what I've done. And it's about what Jesus has done for you and for me. Ultimately the issues explored in this chapter come down to an individual matter, an individual choosing. An old adage puts it succinctly: "Those who are born once will die twice, but those born twice will die but once." Thank You, Jesus, that I need die only once, if at all. That's why I love You. And that's why I celebrate Your great sacrifice in my behalf.

[1] Charles E. Hill, "Atonement in the Apocalypse of John," eds. Charles E. Hill and Frank A. James, III, *The Glory of the Atonement: Biblical, Historical and Practical Perspectives* (Downers Grove, Ill.: InterVarsity Press, 2004), p. 191.

[2] G. K. Beale, *The Book of Revelation: A Commentary on the Greek Text* (Grand Rapids: William B. Eerdmans, 1999), p. 191.

[3] Ty Gibson, *See With New Eyes: The True Beauty of God's Character* (Nampa, Idaho: Pacific Press Pub. Assn., 2000), p. 68.

[4] See *ibid.*, pp. 69, 70.

[5] *Ibid.*, p. 70.

[6] See *ibid.*, p. 71.

[7] Simon Wiesenthal, *The Sunflower: On the Possibilities and Limits of Forgiveness* (New York: Schocken Books, 1998).

[8] Gibson, p. 71.

[9] *Time,* Nov. 4, 1993.

[10] Charles R. Swindoll, *Living Beyond the Daily Grind: Book I* (Dallas: Word Publishing,

1988), p. 113.

[11] Gibson, p. 76.

[12] *Ibid.*

[13] *Ibid.*, p. 77.

[14] John R. W. Stott, *The Cross of Christ* (Downers Gtove, Ill.: InterVarsity Press, 1986), p. 76.

[15] Gibson, p. 78.

[16] Ellen G. White, *The Desire of Ages,* p. 687.

[17] Stott, p. 77.

[18] *Ibid.*, p. 79.

[19] David E. Aune, *Revelation 1-5* (Dallas: Word Books, 1997), p. 47.

[20] Hill, p. 192.

[21] *Ibid.*

[22] *Ibid.*, p. 207.

[23] *Ibid.*, 206.

[24] Johnson, p. 85.

[25] Grant R. Osborne, *Revelation* (Grand Rapids: Baker Academic, 2002), p. 180.

[26] Ellen White tells us that even the righteous wonder if they will be able to stand when Christ appears in clouds of glory, but are assured that Christ's grace is sufficient: "Before his presence, 'all faces are turned into paleness;' upon the rejecters of God's mercy falls the terror of eternal despair. 'The heart melteth, and the knees smite together,' 'and the faces of them all gather blackness.' [Jer. 30:6; Nahum 2:10] The righteous cry with trembling, 'Who shall be able to stand?' The angels' song is hushed, and there is a period of aweful silence. Then the voice of Jesus is heard, saying, 'My grace is sufficient for you.' The faces of the righteous are lighted up, and joy fills every heart. And the angels strike a note higher, and sing again, as they draw still nearer the earth" (*The Great Controversy,* p. 641).

[27] Ellen G. White, *Gospel Workers,* p. 148.

CHAPTER 3

I LOVE JESUS BECAUSE . . .

HE KNOWS MY NAME

The (Lamb's) Book of the Living
Revelation 3:5; 13:8

It was as if God and Satan were playing cards for souls. If Amon, the prison commandant, won, his friend Oskar would pay him 7,400 złoty. If he hit a natural, it would be 14,800 złoty. "But if I win," Oskar said, "then you give me Helen for my list."

The commandant wanted to think about that. Helen Hirsch was his private maid there at Emalia prison camp near Crakow, Poland. It wasn't that he really cared about the woman. Lena, as he called her, lived in constant fear of him. SS Hauptsturmführer Amon Goeth could kill in an instant. The slightest misstep would unleash brutal fury. She'd seen him kill. In fact, she'd been marched off to the firing squad more than once, only to have him change his mind at the last minute. Most of the time Helen simply wanted to die. But life is life, and something in her clung to it no matter the terrifying uncertainty.

"Come on," Oskar urged. "She's going to Auschwitz anyhow." But Amon was so used to Helen that he couldn't easily wager her away. When he'd thought of an end for her, it had probably always been that he would finish her by his own hand. If he played cards for her and lost, he would be under pressure, as a Viennese sportsman, to give up the pleasure of intimate murder.

Oskar got up from the table and bustled around Amon's room, looking for stationery with an official letterhead on it. He wrote out the marker for Amon to sign should he lose: "I authorize that the name of prisoner Helen Hirsch be added to any list of skilled workers relocated with Herr Oskar Schindler's DEF Works."

Amon, the dealer in this morbid hand of blackjack, gave Oskar an 8 and a 5. Oskar asked to be dealt more. He received a 5 and an ace. It would have to do. Then Amon began dealing more cards to himself. A 4 came up, and then a king. "God in heaven," Amon muttered. He seemed to be too fastidious to use obscenities. "I'm out." He laughed a little though, not really amused. "My first cards," he explained, "were a 3 and a 5. With a 4 I figured I'd need another card. Then I got this king."

In the end, Amon signed the marker. Oskar picked up all the chits he'd won that evening from him and returned them. "Just look after the girl for me," he said, "till it's time for us all to leave."

Out in the kitchen, Helen Hirsch did not know that she'd been saved through a card game.

Probably because Oskar reported his evening with Amon to his trusted Jewish accountant Itzhak Stern, rumors of Oskar's plan soon spread. There was a Schindler's list. More than a mere tabulation of names, it was a matter of life and death. In the end more than a thousand names would be carefully typed into it. Only those included in Oskar's dozen pages of names had a future. Rumor had it, too, that he was paying for every name on his list.[1]

The book of Revelation also tells of a list with names on it. It is the one list in all the universe that spells the difference between eternal life and unending death.[2] Revelation calls it "the book of life": "And I saw the dead, the great and the small, standing before the throne, and books were opened; and another book was opened, which is *the book* of life; and the dead were judged from the things which were written in the books, according to their deeds. . . . And if anyone's name was not found written in the book of life, he was thrown into the lake of fire" (Rev. 20:12-15, NASB; cf. Rev. 3:5). Elsewhere in the Apocalypse we find that the "book of life" belongs to the Lamb:[3] "nothing unclean, and no one who practices abomination and lying, shall ever come into it [the Holy City, New Jerusalem], but only those whose names are written in the Lamb's book of life" (Rev. 21:27, NASB). "All who dwell on the earth will worship him [the beast], *everyone* whose name has not been written from the foundation of the world in the book of life of the Lamb who has been slain" (Rev. 13:8, NASB).

The Lamb has a list. And it is a list *of life.*

I have an artist's rendering of Jesus and His life-promising list that I regularly use (as part of a PowerPoint presentation) when I speak on

REVELATION'S GREAT LOVE STORY

Revelation's great judgment and atonement themes. As I write, it is the wallpaper for both my desk and laptop computers. It has a marbled burgundy background, rich yet soft, almost pastel. The bottom margin is wispy white, like a cloud. There Jesus sits, dressed in a soft white robe that stands out sharply against the wine-toned background but nearly blurs with the colorless cloud on which He appears to be sitting. Jet-black, neatly groomed hair and beard sharpen the contrasts, as well as do the flesh tones of His face and hands.

You expect Jesus to be looking at you, but He's totally absorbed, gazing down with an expression of satisfaction on His face. An oversized book covers His lap. While I know that the word Revelation uses for the book of life is more likely that referring to a scroll than a modern bound book, every time I see this picture I think of the book in it as the book of life. The volume is thick, like an old library dictionary that needs a strong wooden stand for support. The ancient leather binding with its raised reliefs and gilt-edged pages give a classy limited edition production feel. It takes both hands to hold. One hand keeps the heavy volume tipped up so that Jesus can read. The other is holding on to the edge of one of its pages, as if He is lingering just a little longer on something before He turns it. Embossed bolded words on the spine say it all: Book of Life.

Every time I see that picture, I view Jesus in a new way and understand the book of Revelation even more. This is *His* book—a registry of those from every nation whom He "purchased for God" with His blood (Rev. 5:9, NASB; cf. Rev. 13:8). There Jesus sits, lovingly reading name after name. Absorbed. Satisfied. Protective. I imagine Him recalling experiences that put those names there, making it a book of remembrance (Mal. 3:16-18). As He sees all that His soul-crushing death on the cross has accomplished, He is truly satisfied (Isa. 53:11; cf. Heb. 12:2). Perhaps His book goes with Him wherever He does. He's not about to leave it or forget it. It's too precious. Jesus will brag on every name there to the Father and His angels (Rev. 3:5).

Because the Lamb's book of life is a list that He keeps with my name in it, I pretend the page He's lingering on has my name on it—Larry Lee Lichtenwalter. The smile on His face is because He's looking at my name. He's remembering how it got there and is happy that it's there. So am I.

Can You Spell My Name?

The first biblical mention of a book of life occurs in the golden calf incident, when Moses asked God to "blot me out of the book you have written" (Ex. 32:32, NIV) if He would not forgive the nation.[4] God Himself called the volume "my book" (verse 33). In doing so He represents Himself as having a record of all who are under His special care and guardianship. The imagery derives from the ancient custom (both in the Old Testament and the Greco-Roman worlds) of keeping genealogical records (see Neh. 7:5, 64; 12:22, 23) and of enrolling citizens for various purposes (Jer. 22:30; Eze. 13:9). Scripture mentions a register of the citizens of Israel (Ps. 9:5; 87:6; Isa. 4:3). Evidently the Israelites who came up out of Egypt were entered in a muster roll of the living citizens. Moses knew his name was there. Ezekiel called such a list "the writing of the house of Israel" (Eze. 13:9). Those who died had their names erased each year. To have one's name removed from a register book would indicate loss of citizenship.

Especially relevant is the heavenly book containing the names of the righteous (Ps. 69:28; Dan. 12:1). Messianic prophecies pointed to an eschatological (end-time) register of those who would be citizens of the renewed Jerusalem (Isa. 4:3; Dan. 12:1).[5] Thus Scripture uses a social practice—keeping record of the names of those who were citizens of a particular city or group—to help us understand heavenly and eschatological realities. The custom illustrated and pointed to something more significant in the heavenly realm. People could grasp the truths conveyed. Revelation employs this same social tradition to illustrate and point to something more significant in the heavenly realm when it uses "book of life" imagery.

Such city or group registers were more than mere tabulation. They listed names of real individuals.

Names are significant and powerful. The way we speak of our friends, spouses, children, and coworkers matters both to them and us. Our use of names communicates both positive and negative feelings. Whenever our name appears in print, we check to see if it is spelled correctly. And we look to make sure our name is on some important list—an overbooked flight, a special banquet, an announcement of public recognition or extraordinary opportunity. We feel a strange kind of devaluation when we're not included on some desirable list, or our names are publicaly mispronounced or even made fun of.

The ability to identify others by their names is a major asset in almost every area of life. Saying a name is the first word we speak in starting a conversation or establishing a relationship. It sets a tone and initiates the relationship. One of the initial ways of demonstrating respect for others is to learn the names (and labels) they have been given or have chosen for themselves and to use them in a respectful way.[6]

Because a name becomes a part of human identity, it cannot be changed at whim without disturbing the inner substance of the individual.[7] The Hebrew people understood more deeply than we do the connection between identity and a name. Every name was significant. More than a title, it conveyed the very nature of the person. It was a clue to character—so much so that it was essential to change one's name if one's character altered.[8]

Thus to have your name on a list was to *be* on the list.

Sometimes I wonder why people don't know my name or who I am, especially in my small community of Berrien Springs. We come and go in some of the same places. Although I pastor the second-largest congregation of my denomination church in the community (and local conference) and write books, I am still unknown by name or face, even by some well-placed denominational leaders. Some have heard my name but don't know my face. Others have seen my face but have no idea of the name that goes with it. Either way, I'm not known. And the reverse is also true. There are so many right around me whose names I don't know—children, their parents, students, even a few colleagues in ministry. There are names I can hardly pronounce and many I have not even learned to spell correctly.

I like my name. L.A.R.R.Y. L.E.E. L.I.C.H.T.E.N.W.A.L.T.E.R. Lichtenwalter is 13 letters long. It gets misspelled and mispronounced all the time. Sometimes people think my last name is Walter and my first name is Lichten. And others switch it around, assuming that my first name is Walter and my last Lichten. I force people to learn how to spell my name by making it part of my e-mail address—the whole 13-letter thing. I figure if you want to send me an e-mail bad enough, you need to know how to spell my name. I also help people learn how to pronounce it (at least the anglicized way—my German friends don't have any problems). Lick (like you are licking a lollipop). Ten (you are licking 10 lollipops). Walter (that one should be easy). Now say it: "Lick—10—Walter."

Revelation's imagery of the Lamb's book of life assures me that Jesus knows my name. It is written down in His book. Because it's on His list, He knows how it's spelled (and pronounced). Most of all, He knows *me*. Not just my legal label, but the inner *me*. I matter to Jesus. I am important to Him. To have your name on the list is to *be* on the list! That's why I love Jesus—He knows my name (me), and my name is (I am) on His list. Jesus loves and cares for me. John knew that. That's why he loved Jesus too. And that's why he tells us about this wonderful list that Jesus keeps and likes to read—the list of life. Jesus wants everyone to know about His book and have their names written there too!

Heavenly Passport

On page 1 of my U.S. passport—right across from the inside cover that bears my picture, passport number, and other important data—there's an authoritative sentence addressed to every other nation I might visit: "The Secretary of State of the United States of America hereby requests all whom it may concern to permit the citizen/national of the United States named herein to pass without delay or hindrance and in case of need to give all lawful aid and protection." I show my blue passport with pride wherever I travel.

Many complain about the bureaucratic hassles of U.S. Customs and Passport Control at our international airports. It can be intimidating with all the lines and waiting, the presence of guns and sniffing dogs, the scanning of passports and security cameras monitoring every move. Officials look at your picture, then at you, then at your picture again, then the computer screen. Hesitating, thinking—about you. Glancing over and seeing people having their picture taken and being fingerprinted, you try to act as if it doesn't matter. But you keep eyeing the official behind the counter to assure yourself that everything's OK. So the Passport Control agent's sudden smile and words of welcome are good news. As I take my documents back with a light heart, I realize that I'm in—home! It's good to be home in the U.S.A. no matter the technicalities. I am an American and I have the papers to prove it. As I head to retrieve my luggage on the baggage claim carousel, I wonder about those still back at Passport Control in the longer visitor lines. Especially those whose documents don't allow the privileges that mine do. Some will have a lot of explaining to do in order to get in. They will have electronic fingerprinting to match. And some will never make it.

Revelation assures me that the Lamb's book of life is my passport to the kingdom of God with its eternal city called the New Jerusalem (Rev. 20:15; 21:27).

The descent of the New Jerusalem is the last prophetic event of the Apocalypse (Rev. 21:1-22:5). The arrival of the Holy City gives the fulfillment of all hopes, the answer to all the world's longings, the quenching of all thirsts (Rev. 21:6). Its coming will forever remove seven of humanity's enemies: the sea,[9] death, mourning, crying, pain, night, and the curse

(Rev. 21:1, 4, 25; 22:3, 4). God makes everything new (Rev. 21:5). The former painful things that we human beings have experienced on earth are forever gone (verse 4).

We could encapsulate the deeply personal and existential nature of this grand moment in the imagery of God gently taking a handkerchief and wiping away all tears (every tear) from every citizen-saint of this city of light and life (Rev. 21:4; cf. Rev. 7:17; Isa. 25:8; 35:10; 65:19). The context suggests that God accounts for the wounds of the past[10]—that He acknowledges what His people have gone through and takes our experience seriously. This healing is both individual and relational. Here the human family—and all the families of the earth—finds both blessing and final reconciliation, because "the leaves of the tree of life [are] for the healing of the nations" (Rev. 22:2).[11] God removes all national and linguistic barriers and alienation. Humanity is now united in one family, its members at peace with one another and God.

No greater statement of the end of one kind of moral existence and the beginning of a new one can be found in Scripture.[12]

The vision of the New Jerusalem continues with a few details from the center of the city: throne, river, and tree (Rev. 22:1-5). The nearer one gets to the center of the city, the less like a city it seems and the more like a garden, something surpassing the original Garden of Eden. The allusion to Eden is intentional. Revelation transplants the rich soil of the original garden, envisioning a cosmopolis of paradise, not a garden per se but a city in which the tree of life stands and in which God and the Lamb are present.[13] The vision ends with a promise of its certainty and invitations to participate in it (verses 6, 17).

Even the best words cannot describe the realities, because they are beyond imagination. John attempted to put in writing what writing cannot contain. But it is enough. Based on what he does communicate, who would not want to be here? Something in every one of us resonates with the incredible imagery even as we debate which parts of the vision are symbolic and what exactly the various pictures mean. We know that it focuses on perfect access to God and Christ, offering fellowship with God and others unhindered either by sin or by the limits imposed by living in a fallen world. It assures us that all marks of the Fall will be erased forever and promises the resurrection of our loved ones. God will give us life eternal and perfect peace and will deliver us from sorrow and death. Would you like to be there? This is the place to be! Being a citizen of this city is an infinite privilege.

The book of Revelation makes it very clear that the only ones with access to the Holy City are "those whose names are written in the Lamb's book of life" (Rev. 21:27, NASB). So if you're on His list, you get it. But more than that, you belong there. The book of life is no temporary visa but a passport. Ultimately one's name on the Lamb's list has to do with being a citizen of the Holy City.

We have already noted how Scripture uses a social practice—keeping record of the names of those who are citizens or belong to a particular city or group—to help us understand heavenly realities. With its book of life imagery, Revelation assures us that something really happens at the administrative center of God's universal government when we accept Jesus Christ as our Savior. We become a citizen of His kingdom (cf. Phil. 3:20). Our liberation from the kingdom of darkness and our incorporation into the kingdom of God is not only celebrated in heaven but recorded in the book of life (cf. Luke 15:7, 10, 11-32; 10:20).[14] As my friend Angel Rodriguez writes: "The reality of the book of life underscores for the people of God the fact that those who belong to Christ are already members of the heavenly city, of the kingdom of God. Their names are already written in the heavenly ledger, and they are considered to be citizens of the kingdom, with all the privileges, prerogatives, and responsibilities that entails. The certainty of their heavenly citizenship is so unquestionable that Jesus encourages them to rejoice because their names are already in the book of life. The certainty of that act is also emphasized by insisting that it is God Himself who writes the names in the book and that this takes place in heaven, out of the reach of human envy and evil powers. Whatever may happen to the name recorded in heaven will be the result of the decision of a loving God."[15]

Revelation depicts the implications of the Lamb's book of life through images that have to do with our identity, citizenship, and moral orientation. The Apocalypse isn't concerned as much about *what* is going to happen in the end and *when* it is going to take place as it is with *who* the people of God are and how they are to be understood within those events and time.[16] Thus Revelation deals with such issues as who we are as God's people in relation to the world, to angelic beings, and to God. It answers who we are in contrast with those from Babylon, those who dwell on the earth, and those who are forever outside the city. Clearly our moral and spiritual orientation resides elsewhere—with the Lamb whom we are to passionately follow and with the holiness of the city of which we are already a part (Rev. 14:1-5; 21:27; 22:15; 17:14). The name of God, the name of His

Holy City, and even Christ's new name are now part of our identity and vision (Rev. 3:12). Notice here an ABA pattern in that the name of God and the name of Christ frame the name of the eschatological city.[17] The city is defined by the Father and the Son. Their names and the city's name then define the people upon whom they are written.

The imagery of the Lamb's list and the access to the Eternal City is a wonderful picture of stability and security.[18] The believer is a citizen of heaven no matter what the forces of evil do.[19] Here is awesome assurance!

When I was a teenager in love, I used to do the daisy petal thing. "She loves me. She loves me not. She loves me. She loves me not." And so on, until I had pulled off the last petal. Like everyone else, I hoped the final petal was a lucky one—"She loves me!" Sometimes we wonder about salvation and eternity. *Am I saved? Or not?* we muse. So we pull the petals in our imagination, the petal of each day reflecting our circumstances, failures, victories, and emotions. "I'm saved. I'm not saved. I'm saved. I'm not saved. What will the last pull indicate—saved or not?" The Lamb's list delivers us from such anxious uncertainty to sweet assurance, confidence, and peace. If I'm on the list, I'm saved. I don't need to tug at any more petals.

Jesus tells me that I can rejoice because my name is in the heavenly book (Luke 10:20). The greatest joy in the world comes in knowing that your name is included in God's heavenly book, giving you a place in His eternal kingdom. Such knowledge can be the cause of "continuous joy,"[20] as the form of the Greek suggests. This is why I love Jesus. My name in His book is assuring!

The Man Comes Around

Shortly before his death Johnny Cash sang in his melancholy way an apocalyptic composition that he entitled "The Man Comes Around." It's a song about the sobering moment of judgment somewhere up ahead that will hold every one of us accountable for how we have lived. "There's a man goin' 'round takin' names," he pines. It's a sobering thought—God taking down names and keeping records of deeds and character. As Cash said, it can make the hair on your arms stand up.

The book of Revelation refers to heaven's record books: "And I saw the dead, the great and the small, standing before the throne, and books were opened; . . . and the dead were judged from the things which were written in the books, according to their deeds" (Rev. 20:12, NASB). The truth of the judgment is that everyone who has ever lived will be rewarded according to what they have done (Rev. 20:12, 13; 22:12; 2:23; 18:6).

While salvation is by grace alone, the doctrine of judgment teaches us that character and life in the end will be the test of the fruit of the tree (Rev. 2:23; 22:12; cf. Matt. 7:16, 20; 10:32-33; 25:31-46; John 15:6; Rom. 2:9, 10; 2 Cor. 5:10).

The book of Revelation is a text filled with the imagery of eyes. John sees God's throne and around it "four living creatures full of eyes in front and behind" (Rev. 4:6, NASB) (" . . . around and within" [verse 8, NASB]). He beholds Jesus, who possesses "eyes like a flame of fire" (Rev. 2:18, NASB). Jesus is the lamb with "seven eyes" that are the spirits sent out into the earth (Rev. 5:6). Roaming the earth, those spirits not only gaze in every direction, they size up and take stock of everything.[21] Each of the messages to the seven churches begins with an examination: "I know" what you're doing, where you live, the trouble you're having, etc. (Rev. 2:2, 9, 19; 3:1, 8, 15). In the end, all will know that Jesus is one "who searches the minds and hearts" and will give to each according as their works deserve (Rev. 2:23). In the world of the Apocalypse one is either seen or threatened with exposure (Rev. 3:18; 16:15).[22] All things are recorded and ultimately revealed in judgment. The sense of being watched by apocalyptic paparazzi lingers long after you finish reading the book.

God obviously takes us seriously. Every moment, every act, every thought at any time or anywhere, passes before the eyes of one who searches the heart and mind. In the end, God takes our freedom and choice seriously. He will honor our choices even when they are against Him and the meaning of true life. The call to "fear God" because of our account-ability to Him is both an Old and New Testament reality: "The conclusion, when all has been heard, *is:* fear God and keep His commandments, because this *applies to* every person. For God will bring every act to judgment, everything which is hidden, whether it is good or evil" (Eccl. 12:13, 14, NASB). "For we must all appear before the judgment seat of Christ, so that each one may be recompensed for his deeds in the body, according to what he has done, whether good or bad" (2 Cor. 5:10, NASB). "Fear God and give glory to Him, for the hour of His judgment has come" (Rev. 14:7, NKJV). Not only does Scripture remind us that God takes us seriously—it also calls us to take God seriously.

It is no accident that the Lamb's list appears alongside heaven's record books: "And I saw the dead, the great and the small, standing before the throne, and books were opened; and another book was opened, which is *the book* of life; and the dead were judged from the things which were written in the books, according to their deeds. . . . And if anyone's name was not found written in the book of life, he was thrown into the lake of fire" (Rev. 20:12-15, NASB). While people are justly judged according to their works, only those inscribed in the Lamb's book of life will escape the lake of fire. This is significant. Despite the dramatic events of Revelation 20—Satan's 1,000-year imprisonment, the first resurrection privileges of reigning with Christ and liberation from second death power, Gog and Magog's final siege of the saints in the Holy City upon his release, the devouring lake of fire and the final destruction of Satan, and the great white throne judgment at which what one has done is both recorded and counts—the greater focus of Revelation's millennium drama is on the book of life. Apparently it decides the ultimate issues of moral accountability and divine judgment. Coming as it does as almost an aside at the chapter's close, it may be easy to miss. But here after all the spectacular events listed above, the book of life looms large. The most important truth (and document) of the ages, it is the deciding factor of human destiny and history, serving both as a witness against those whose names are *not found* written in it and as a passport to the Eternal City for those whose names *are found* written there.

Judgment examines the books—what one has done or not done. But it also involves the book of life. "Is their name written there in the Lamb's list?" That's the ultimate question. Only for those whose names appear in this book will the judgment mean joyful vindication rather than shameful destruction.

As I read these things, I wonder, *How can the mere appearance of one's name in the book of life counterbalance the damning evidence contained in the book of our deeds (Rev. 20:12)?*[23]

Revelation elsewhere reminds us that this deciding book belongs to the Lamb who has been slain in sacrifice for those listed in it (Rev. 13:8; cf. Rev. 21:27). Schindler's list cost Schindler dearly. It bankrupted him. But the drama of his courage and cunning pales beside the price paid for each name inscribed in the Lamb's list of life (Rev. 5:9; cf. 1 Peter 1:18-20). As we have seen, Revelation refers to this book as the "*Lamb's* book of life" (Rev. 21:27), clearly linking it with the cross. The book belongs to "the Lamb who has been slain" (Rev. 13:8, NASB).[24] Substitutionary atonement and mediation are assumed. Robes (character and life) are whitened by the blood shed there (Rev. 7:14; 22:14). The cross made the book of life possible, for it was the slain Lamb that became the sacrifice for sin and enabled the people of God to have life.[25]

The juxtaposition of the "book of life" and the "books" takes us to the heart of the pre-Advent judgment that forever vindicates those who profess Christ. Ellen White tells us that "when we become children of God, our names are written in the Lamb's book of life, and they remain there until the time of the investigative judgment. Then the name of every individual will be called, and his record examined, by Him who declares, 'I know thy works.' If in that day it shall appear that all our wicked deeds have not been fully repented of, our names will be blotted from the book of life, and our sins will stand against us."[26] Elsewhere we read that "the book of life contains the names of all who have ever entered the service of God. If any of these depart from Him, and by stubborn persistence in sin become finally hardened against the influences of His Holy Spirit, their names will in the judgment be blotted from the book of life, and they themselves will be devoted to destruction."[27]

Jesus alludes to the possibility of names removed from the book of life when He affirms His commitment to overcomers in Sardis: "I will not erase his name from the book of life" (Rev. 3:5, NASB). The force of the Greek double negative (*ouv mh*), however, asserts that Jesus "will *never* blot out their names." We find here more than a warning against apostasy. The book seeks to assure, not to distress. But the possibility exists, for the promise of names never being erased is meaningless if the "blotting out" could never occur at all.[28] Both Moses and David knew that possibility, that certainty and accountability can hang side by side in the divine way of things (Ex. 32:32, 33; Ps. 69:28). In the end, only those who remain faithful will have their names stay on the Lamb's list. Participation depends on Christ's sacrificial death and our faithful perseverance in Him. Both aspects must remain intact.[29]

Such talk leads many to begin pulling daisy petals once again ("I'm saved, I'm not saved, I'm . . ."), yanking away any assurance they might have had. We know that a person's works are an unmistakable mark of where their loyalties lie, and that the record books are in a sense *vouchers* to support what is in or not in the book of life.[30] But even then the focus is not on deeds per se but on whether one's name is indeed there on the Lamb's list (Rev. 20:15). If we carefully reread Ellen White's comments above, we will see that any erasing of names from the book of life comes in the context of sins that have not been repented of (and subsequently unconfessed). She writes of departing from Christ and of stubborn persistence in sin as well as of resisting the voice of the Holy Spirit. It is not a matter of measuring up but of choice, of being in Christ. Scripture is very clear: "If we confess our sins, He [God] is faithful and righteous to forgive us our sins and cleanse us from all unrighteousness" (1 John 1:9, NASB). This confession (with its implied repentance) is not just of sin, but by its very nature is an acknowledgment of Jesus as the Lamb who takes away the sins of the world (John 1:29, 36). When we believe with the heart and confess with the mouth that Jesus is Lord, we are saved (Rom. 10:9-11). The focus is on so identifying with the substitutionary death of Christ that we have washed ourselves in the Lamb's blood (Rev. 7:14; 22:14). The record books simply give evidence of such identity with Christ's atoning work.

Thus remaining faithful to Christ means clinging to Him as the Lamb who takes away the sins of the world. Again, Revelation refers to the "book of life" as the "the Lamb's book of life" and clearly links it with the cross (Rev. 21:27; 13:8). In other words, inclusion in both depends on Christ's sacrificial death and our faithful perseverance in Christ. Both aspects must remain intact. When both aspects are indeed preserved, we can rejoice because of the certainty that God will pronounce judgment in our favor (Rev. 18:20; Dan. 7:22). Christ has died and paid the price, and His blood cleanses thoroughly. When we receive Him as Savior and come to Him for cleansing, He indeed cleanses us and writes our names in His book. As long as we remain in Him, daily washing ourselves in His blood (Rev. 22:14),[31] nothing will ever erase our names. Thus we find more assurance here than any warning (Rev. 3:5).

Once Moses pleaded for God to remove his name from His book—that he might die rather than that Israel should perish. "Please blot me out from Your book which You have written," he begged (Ex 32:32, NASB; cf. Ps. 69:28). We can only imagine that awesome moment of human intercession. Scripture tells us that it took place the day after the people of God danced around the golden calf (Ex. 32:30). As the enormity of the people's transgression dawned upon him with startling shocking reality, he ached. So intensely evil did their sin appear that he questioned whether there could be any pardon. Nothing could be said in their favor. It was a terrible thing they had done. But then he pleaded: "But now, if You will, forgive their sin—but if not, please blot me out" (verse 32, NASB).

In the process of it all Moses' mind wrestled with the great theme of atonement through the sacrifice of innocent lambs. God had indicated that He would accept a blameless substitute in the place of a just death for sin. The deep possibilities in the law of substitution stirred his heart. And so he offered, "Blot me out! Let them live, but blot me out." Moses was willing to surrender his own life, if that would serve to atone for their sin. He would bear their guilt in order to secure their forgiveness, thus literally standing in the breach before God in behalf of an unworthy, sinful people who forgot their Savior who had brought them out of the slavery of Egypt (Ps. 106:19-23). The Lord responded by saying that the judgment would hold each person accountable for his or her own deeds. A human being cannot possibly make an atonement for another's sins. Yet God did offer a promise. While the Lord would not accept Moses' offer, He did give Israel more time to learn, to repent, to grow, to decide, to be forgiven, and to be restored to fellowship with Him.

Moses prefigures Christ, who at another time went into the garden and then ascended Calvary to make an atonement for our sin.[32] As Moses struggled with the weight of Israel's sins, Jesus struggled with the weight of the sin of the world—our sins. In His intercession at Gethsemane, in every step to the cross, in every experience on the cross, in that darkness surrounding the cross when He cried out, "My God, My God, why have You forsaken Me?" (Matt. 27:45, NKJV), Jesus was saying to the Father, "Blot Me! Blot Me instead of them! Let Me taste the horrors of hell that they might taste the sweetness of the tree of life. Let Me endure the weight of condemnation that they may experience the joy of acceptance by You. Let Me die that they might live. Let their disobedience be Mine, My obedience theirs. Blot Me, Father. Blot Me!"

And as Jesus hung on the cross it was true substitution. His hands were nailed for what our hands have done and His feet for where our feet have walked. There He felt the alienation from the Father for all we have ever done. "Blot Me! Blot Me!" Jesus says. And He died. For you and for me—so that our names might be registered in His book of the living.

I believe that those whose names are entered into that book and remain there forever are those individuals who forever have a distinct, intelligent knowledge of what their salvation cost. That is why they dip their robes in the blood of the Lamb and follow the Lamb in sacrificial life—surrendered in a holy rhythm of obedience to the Father. They overcome "by the blood of the Lamb" (Rev. 12:11). The reason for their victory over the world is the death of Jesus and their conscious choice to identify with it.[33] Such people need never fear the judgment.

Not Valid Unless Signed

In the blockbuster movie *Titanic* the fictional character Jack Dawson won a ticket for passage to New York in a dockside card game just before the ship sailed. His elation skyrocketed as his dreams about returning home to America were fulfilled. Even more, a shipboard romance brought excitement to his life as a drifter. Then tragedy struck. What appeared to be a ticket to complete fulfillment turned into a reservation for death in the icy North Atlantic. The *Titanic* promised safe passage to all ticketed passengers, from first class down. As everyone knows, more drowned than were spared. The promise was false. But there is a divine list of passengers bound for heaven and its Holy City. All who are on the Lamb's list will reach their destination. We can be sure of it.

My passport has another important detail on page 1. Down at the bottom is a simple thin line running from margin to margin. Underneath it are the words "Signature of Bearer." Then centered below the signature line in bold capital letters is: "Not Valid Until Signed."

No matter all the official data on the inside cover page, either about myself or the U.S. government—my passport is not valid unless I have personally identified with it by fixing my signature. Gladly I signed my passport, scribbling my name across the full length of the line. This is my proof of identity as an American citizen.

Revelation makes it clear that within the arena of history, the inclusion of names in the book of life rests on the event of the cross (Rev. 13:8) and appears to take place when the individual surrenders his or her life to the Lord.[34] The "Lamb's book of life" implies a saving relationship with Jesus Christ in which we have personally received the benefits of His death in our behalf and have decided to follow Him as the slain Lamb and King of kings, Lord of lords. By choosing to be "with Him" (Rev. 17:14, NASB), we affix our signature as it were. Our name which has been written in the book of life from the foundation of the world (Rev. 13:8; 17:8) suddenly becomes valid because we have affixed our signature by personally receiving Christ's sacrifice in our behalf. "Not valid until signed!" It's the point in time where predestination and freewill intersect. Where what God ordained and what we choose converge. That's what washing robes in the blood of the Lamb is about. Validating what God ordained before the foundation of the world, it makes us citizens of the Eternal City where He is present and His face is seen.

The greatest joy in the world comes in knowing that Christ has written our name in His heavenly book, that we are assured a place in His eternal kingdom (Luke 10:20). If we have received the Jesus who died for us, we can be sure our name is in His book!

Right now I'm thinking of that picture of Jesus holding that oversized book of life in His lap and lovingly reading name after name. Absorbed. Satisfied. Protective. Because that book has my name in it, I imagine the page He's lingering on has my name listed on it—Larry Lee Lichtenwalter. The smile on His face is because He's looking at my name, remembering how it got there. He's happy my name's there, and so am I. That's why I love Jesus. Not only does He know my name, but He's written it in His special book. That's why John loved Him too. And so can you.

---

[1] Thomas Keneally, *Schindler's List* (New York: Simon and Schuster, 1993), pp. 275-280.

[2] Johnson, *The Triumph of the Lamb,* p. 299.

[3] Osborne, *Revelation,* p. 503.

[4] *Ibid.,* p. 180.

[5] Angel Manuel Rodriguez, "The Heavenly Books of Life and of Human Deeds," *Journal of the Adventist Theological Society,* 13/1 (Spring 2002), p. 11.

[6] David W. Gill, *Doing Right: Practicing Ethical Principles* (Downers Grove, Ill.: InterVarsity Press, 2004), p. 123.

[7] John Shelby Spong and Denise G. Haines, *Beyond Moralism: A Contemporary View of the Ten Commandments* (Morristown, N. J.: Christianity for a Third Millennium, 2000), p. 39.

[8] Gill, p. 138.

[9] In Scripture "sea" has a negative connotation, representing void, darkness, and chaos (Gen. 1:2; Ps. 18:12; Job 26:10; Prov. 8:27), death and "non-being" (Eze. 26:19:21; Jonah 2:6; Hab. 3:10), and evil (Isa. 27:1; 51:9, 10). Revelation also associates the sea with Babylon (Rev. 16:12) and to the origins of the beast (Rev. 13:1; cf. Dan. 7:3). Thus in Scripture sea becomes the metaphoric place of disturbed and stormy social and political conditions out of which the enemies of God's people commonly arise.

[10] Jacques B. Doukhan, *Secrets of Revelation: The Apocalypse Through Hebrew Eyes* (Hagerstown, Md.: Review and Herald Pub. Assn., 2002), p. 194.

[11] Stefanovic, *Revelation of Jesus Christ,* on Rev. 22:3.

[12] Easley, *Revelation,* p. 395.

[13] William P. Brown, *The Ethos of the Cosmos: The Genesis of Moral Imagination in the Bible* (Grand Rapids: William B. Eerdmans, 1999), p. 228.

[14] Rodriguez, p. 18.

[15] *Ibid.*

[16] Edith M. Humphrey, "A Tale of Two Cities and (At Least) Three Women," ed. David L. Barr, *Reading the Book of Revelation: A Resource for Students* (Atlanta: Society of Biblical Literature, 2003), p. 82.

[17] Osborne, p. 199.

[18] Easley, p. 58.

[19] Osborne, p. 503.

[20] Darrell L. Block, *Luke* (Grand Rapids: Zondervan, 1996), p. 294.

[21] In Zechariah 4:10 the "seven eyes of the Lord . . . range throughout the earth." It points to the Lamb's ability to see what happens throughout the world and to act powerfully wherever He chooses.

[22] Harry O. Maier, *Apocalypse Recalled: The Book of Revelation After Christendom* (Minneapolis: Fortress Press, 2002), p. 64.

[23] Johnson, p. 85.

[24] Osborne, p. 180.

[25] *Ibid.,* p. 503.

[26] Ellen G. White, *Signs of the Times,* Aug. 6, 1885.

[27] Ellen G. White, *Patriarchs and Prophets,* p. 326.

[28] Osborne, p. 183.

[29] *Ibid.,* p. 180.

[30] Robert L. Thomas, *Revelation 8-22: An Exegetical Commentary* (Chicago: Moody Press, 1995), p. 432.

[31] The form of the Greek "those who wash their robes" is a present active participle, implying an ongoing repeated experience rather than a once for all one.

[32] Ellen G. White, *Patriarchs and Prophets,* p. 326.

[33] See Beale, p. 436.

[34] Rodriguez, p. 14.

CHAPTER 4

I LOVE JESUS BECAUSE . . .

HE'S BUSY IN MY WORLD

Where Things Really Happen
Revelation 1:9-20

One of the haunting images I have of Lisbon, Portugal, is *Cristo Rei*—*Christ the King*—a colossal stone statue of Jesus Christ on a towering concrete base reaching some hundreds of feet above sea level. The enormous sculpture stands to the west across the Tagus River facing the capital. Sprawling Lisbon flows up from the river like a curved amphitheater into the rising hills behind it, as if seated there looking across the river to another hill—where Jesus stands, hands outstretched. You can't miss *Cristo Rei*, day or night!

Every evening I went to the open window of my tenth-floor hotel room and looked past the high-rise buildings and neon lights to this uplifted Jesus. I could view traffic moving through the city and sense the bustle of Lisbon's nightlife. Voices from the street below would catch my ear, as well as the hum of ventilation fans, traffic, and an occasional barking dog. The cool night air brushed against my face. There in the distance was Jesus, bathed in iridescent light—almost silhouetted against the night sky. Facing this centuries-old city of explorers and merchants now filled with advanced twenty-first-century occupants, arms outstretched, it was as if He were saying, "I am here. Right here in Lisbon with you. Can you see Me? Look! Live every day conscious of My abiding presence right where you live."

But I wondered how many really thought anything about *Cristo Rei*. How many days could go by without their even noticing this towering

Revelation's Great Love Story

Christ except as a place to point tourists, an unmissable landmark when giving directions or finding one's way. Or a place to take one's children on a day off, climbing to its high observation deck at the foot of Jesus for a view of Lisbon from the other side of the river.

Each night I would go to bed haunted with the reality that most Lisboans spent much of every day with eyes and minds focused on details about deadlines, delays, money, dress, food and shelter, work and recreation, politics, and more. In the morning they would get up and shower, dress, eat, work, buy, sell, worry, hurt and be hurt, make love, drink themselves drunk, enjoy fancy pastries, live for the next pleasure, go hungry, hate, be alone, be afraid, die—everything that happens in a city. Surely Jesus was not really there—not where life really happened. How could He be? After all, monuments are only symbolic, aren't they? This couldn't be real.

Further north in the Portuguese city of Porto, my nineteenth-floor hotel window opened toward the celebrated city famed for its rich history and port wines. My hotel was on the prominent hill opposite Porto, which lay just a little lower across the river. The terrain sloped downward, steep at times, to the river below. Porto, a beautiful European city with sprawling old structures and orange roof tiles, spread up from the riverfront into surrounding hills on the other side. It was a glorious view. One morning I woke up to a Porto enshrouded in clouds. Below me people were going to work. I could hear them opening their shops, driving their cars, talking. But I couldn't see them, the river, or the city on the other side. Clouds even hid the high tower on the opposite hillside. I was literally above the clouds looking down on a sea of white cotton—the kind of view you get when you fly. I wondered about the mystery of things seen and unseen. Later when the sun had burned the fog away, I could see clearly again, but I was still up there in my room. Removed from the life going on below. Unnoticed. Uninvolved.

Some of us view Jesus in a similar way. He's somewhere above the clouds but not down here where I am. Not where real things happen in my life and world. Not where it makes any real difference about what we're struggling with.

Where Things Really Happen

Patmos is a barren, rocky island in the Aegean Sea roughly 10 miles long and approximately six wide. One of my dreams has been to walk along Patmos' rough, barren coast, find a jagged rocky precipice, and fill my ears with the incessant crash of the Aegean waters against the rocks below. That's how John describes the voice of Jesus: like "the sound of many waters" (Rev. 1:15). The sound of the ocean is commanding. So it is with Jesus. I imagine John sitting there thinking about the the sea and listening. I want to imagine Christ's commanding voice wherever I go.

I've memorized the Apocalypse—all 22 chapters. It takes me about an hour and 40 minutes to repeat it nonstop from memory. I rehearse it regularly when I walk, and I've recited it word for word in a dramatic public presentation. Hearing (or reciting) all of Revelation in one setting is deeply moving and has been one of my most spiritually energizing experiences. Revelation has power. I've seen people moved to tears and filled with hope and joy as they listen. They've discovered things about Jesus, about the Apocalypse, about the struggle between Christ and Satan, that they'd never quite grasped before. It's the blessing the book promises to those who read or hear the words of the prophecy (Rev. 1:3). So one of my dreams has been to find that jagged rocky precipice on Patmos and recite the book from start to finish, trying to imagine all that John saw and experienced.

I've also dreamed of, right there on that barren island, recommitting myself to John's Jesus and the awesome truths found here in the book called Revelation—the truths that God calls us to carry to a lost world. It's something that I already do every time I visit the celebrated Ishtar Gate at Berlin's Pergamon Museum—the very gate Daniel walked through almost every day of his life while a captive administrator in Babylon. I sit there in front of the reconstructed gate of original blue and beige glazed brick reliefs of Babylon's deities and think of Daniel's God. I remember the passing of great empires and the fulfillment of prophecy (Dan. 2:1-45; 7:1-28). That Babylon (and its gods) is gone but that the God of heaven, Daniel's deity, is still very much in control. His eternal kingdom will ultimately both come and prevail. The stone cut out without hands is closer now than at any moment in history to pulverizing the feet of clay mixed with iron. As I sit there on a bench in front of the colorful gate I pray, recommitting myself to preaching the book of Daniel and the prophetic worldview it presents.

That's what I've wanted to do at Patmos, too—to recite the Apocalypse from its opening to its close and let its images haunt my imagination and stir my heart. There I've wanted to reflect on history and the eternal Christ—on all that has happened in our world (for and against Him) since the first century. To pray. To rededicate myself to preaching Revelation and the prophetic worldview it portrays.

REVELATION'S GREAT LOVE STORY

I've looked forward to visiting Patmos for many good reasons (some of which have been realized). But when John first arrived there, I'm sure it must have been discouraging. He was neither a tourist nor a missionary, but an exile—an aging pastor separated from those he loved and longed to help. The Roman authorities had isolated him on an island where his enemies thought for sure his influence would vanish and he would finally die of hardship and distress. "I . . . was on . . . Patmos because of the word of God and the testimony of Jesus," John says (Rev. 1:9, NASB). He was just like every other faithful believer in his day, sharing their suffering and trying to let Christ reign fully in his life no matter what.

Now, Patmos was an actual place with genuine hardship and real isolation. And John was truly there and truly alone. As he experienced actual trouble he found his faith and endurance really being tested.

Patmos was where things were really taking place for John.

And you know what? He tells us that on a very specific day on that very real island—a Sabbath day, in fact[1]—Jesus joined him there on that barren island (verses 9-18).

It's awesome when you think about it—Jesus appears where things are really taking place in John's life. As John beholds a very present and visible Jesus, he observes Him moving in the middle of seven golden lampstands that he later learns represent seven churches (verse 20). At the same time, Jesus holds seven stars in His hand that symbolize the leaders of those churches (verse 20). Then Jesus begins dictating letters. To each of the seven churches Jesus says, "I know . . . I know . . . I know . . ." (Rev. 2:2, 9, 13, 19; 3:1, 8, 15).

Now, John is a microcosm of the church.[2] He presents himself as a brother of his hearers who shares with them a threefold experience: affliction, reign, and endurance. "I am John, your brother," he writes. "In Jesus we are partners in suffering and in the Kingdom and in patient endurance. I was exiled to the island of Patmos for preaching the word of God and speaking about Jesus" (Rev. 1:9, NLT). Thus Revelation begins with John's concrete situation (Rev. 1:9), then shifts to the church's also concrete situation (Rev. 2:1-3:21).

John was literally on a real island with a historic name: Patmos. It was an actual place. And he was an actual person. Likewise, the seven churches were seven historical congregations located in Asia: Ephesus, Smyrna, Pergamum, Thyatira, Sardis, Philadelphia, and Laodicea (Rev. 1:4, 11; 22:16). The whole book of Revelation is a circular letter written to seven specific churches that existed in first-century Asia. Many misreadings of

Revelation have resulted from neglecting the simple fact that it is as much (if not more) a letter as it is apocalyptic prophecy.[3] Those who assume that much of the book was not written for its first-century readers and that only later generations can really understand it will miss one of Revelation's important interpretive keys. Because these seven churches really existed and were each facing unique problems and reacting variously to the problems that they did share, they provide a concrete context for seeing Jesus at work both in our lives and in human history (Rev. 2:1-3:21). These churches (and John's letters) are anchored in human history and provide concrete application of larger moral principles posited and developed elsewhere in Revelation.[4] Here Jesus addresses actual individuals in literal churches situated in geographically locatable cities with notable leaders and with named enemies and particular struggles.[5]

What's the point? The book of Revelation pictures Jesus on the island of Patmos revealing Himself to an imprisoned John. We see Christ walking among the Asian churches holding their leaders in His hand. He is relating both to John where he is and to the church where it is. Jesus is no stone statue, no towering monument perched on a hill. Nor is He somewhere up in the clouds, removed from our life. Rather than being uninvolved and unseeing, He is the Living One, who is an actual part of our lives. We have more than symbolism here!

Ellen White tells us that "one thing will certainly be understood from the study of Revelation—that the connection between God and His people is close and decided,"[6] How could it be clearer? Jesus is always where things really happen—in our everyday lives.

The Time of My Life

Andrews University once asked me to talk about time management to a group of Doctor of Ministry students that had come to the seminary there for a two-week intensive class in leadership. The administration told me that I had two hours. It was the last thing I wanted to do (and needed to do or had time to do), but they kept reminding me that I was a busy pastor of a large congregation who preached, wrote books, did adjunct teaching, conducted funerals, gave Bible studies, visited the sick, spoke at camp meetings, and traveled overseas for leadership and speaking appointments. "How do you do it?" they queried. "Certainly you have something to say about time management. Surely you could find the time for something as important as this."

I began those two hours declaring that we never manage time—we only manage ourselves in time. Time will proceed second by second, minute by minute, hour by hour despite our best efforts to control it. It rolls on in its unrelenting journey. What we do have power over is ourselves.[7] Then I stated that before we decided *what* we wanted *to do* with our time, we needed to decide *who* we wanted *to be* in time. Before I know what to do with my time I must decide who I want to be in time. What to do is never as important as what to be.

Being and time run parallel, I suggested. You likely have never thought of the idea before, as most of those in the class had not. But if you *are* (alive, breathing, living, thinking, feeling, hurting or happy), there is time (at least for you). But if you're *not* (dead or never existed), there's no time at all. *Being* and time go together. To live is to exist in time—with the sense that time moves—so there is also history. Time creates a past, a present, and a future. How we live in time determines both time itself and history. "Who are you in time?" I asked. "It will determine what you do in it. They run side by side."

Revelation is a book about time and history. Jesus tells John: Write "the things which you have seen," "the things which are," "and the things which will take place after these things" (Rev. 1:19, NASB). It's a three-part picture. "The things which you have seen" refers to the vision John just saw of the majestic glorified Jesus Christ (verses 9-18). "The things which are" are the seven churches and their present condition, which Jesus will discuss next (Rev. 2:1-3:21). And "the things which will take place after these things" is the rest of Revelation and refers to future events (Rev. 4:1-22:21).[8] Revelation has past, present, and future aspects of history intertwined throughout its message.[9] Some visions concern near events while others involve the remote future or distant past. Certain visions are historical in that they are anchored in a definable point in history while others provide more of a meaning for history—a philosophy of history. They have either taken place or will take place, but it's not important to know when or where, but simply that it happens and impacts everything else in real time and space. These near and past and future events blend together in a tapestry that conveys a particular biblical worldview that can anchor faith wherever one lives in history.

The phrase "the things which will take place after these things" is an expression from Daniel 2:28, 29, 45, in which the prophet clearly speaks about history and its interrelated but sequential flow of events. Revelation 1:19 clearly draws from Daniel 2[10] and thus is rooted in the historical reality of past, present, and future. The combination of past, present, and future revelation in this verse reminds us that Jesus is the Lord of history (Rev. 1:17; cf. Rev. 22:13).[11] As the "first and the last," He has power over time.[12] But Jesus is not just Lord of history in a symbolic way—He is involved in history itself. He is making a difference where it goes and how it ends and what people are doing and becoming in the flow of time. Nothing happens in time and history (and in our lives) apart from His knowledge and involvement. When it's all over, He will be standing there at the end to meet us.

Revelation contains numerous historicist statements, such as references to: "[God] who is and who was and who is to come" (Rev. 1:4, 8, NASB); "things which must soon take place" (Rev. 1:1, NASB; 22:6, NASB); "the time is near" (Rev. 1:3, NASB; Rev. 22:10, NASB); "I am coming" (Rev. 22:12, NASB); "the first things have passed away" (Rev. 21:4, NASB); "the rest of the dead did not come to life until the thousand years were completed" (Rev. 20:5, NASB); "Your righteous acts have been revealed" (Rev. 15:4, NASB); "time came for the dead to be judged" (Rev. 11:18, NASB); "the first woe is past; behold, two woes are still coming after these things" (Rev. 9:12, NASB); "the kingdom of the world has become *the kingdom* of our Lord and of His Christ; and He will reign forever and ever" (Rev. 11:15), etc.; not to mention references to specific time-frames such as 2300 days, 42 months, or 1,000 years (Rev. 11:2, 3, 11; 12:6, 14; 13:5; 20:2-7).

Time and thus history is the sphere in which we live life. History is the arena of God's activity in human affairs. Thus Revelation assures us that the earth (where we are), time (when things happen), and history (the chronicle and story of what actually happens both when and why) all matter.[13] Because the Apocalypse is a book about choice (Rev. 22:10-15, 17; 1:3; 2:7, 11, 17, 26-29; 3:5, 6, 12, 13, 21, 22; 13:9), it helps us understand the results of our decisions. Who we are (have become) as a result of what we have chosen and how our choices affect both history (personal and world) and eternity (our destiny and that of others) are recurring themes. While Revelation's highly symbolic imagery takes us to the cosmic and global, from ages past to eternity future, from heaven to earth and under the earth, using apparently timeless images and sequences to make its varied points, it is nevertheless grounded in human history and assumes history's flow toward a divinely appointed purpose. It encompasses the whole scope of human time.[14] Because Revelation locates the fulfillment of apocalyptic prophecy within the flow of human history, it is consistent with real human existence.

REVELATION'S GREAT LOVE STORY

t   One of the contributions of biblical thought is the notion of linear time, the idea that time moves in a straight line from one distinct beginning to one distinct end. It contrasts with many pagan faiths and concepts that view time as circular, cyclical, something that constantly returns to its beginnings and goes through all the cycles again and again, thus never ending. Pagans spoke of prophetic diviners and deities who recounted the past, present, and future, but Jewish people and Christians recognized that only the true God reveals past, present, and future to His servants (Isa. 42:9; 48:5-7). The book of Revelation reveals Jesus as genuinely in control of history. Because He is Lord of history, He is in charge of our heritage, present situation, and ultimate destiny.

Only a biblical historicism correctly locates the fulfillment of apocalyptic prophecy within the flow of salvation history. It alone is consistent with real life, because it shows the work of Christ in the past, the present, and the future. Thus it alone strengthens our faith. We must be careful, though, how we try to make Revelation "fit" into history. We must determine historical fulfillments by their Christ-centeredness in accordance with the biblical perspective of history.[15] No matter one's view on the historical and sequential nature of Revelation, its broad moral and spiritual principles nevertheless stand within an implied temporality. This historical perspective is most true to human life and enables us to understand some of Revelation's moral and spiritual issues that we otherwise might overlook or deem inconsequential. As a result we realize that Jesus is at work not just in our world, but in human history. The prophetic waymarks are there for us to gain perspective and have hope, but the larger picture of Jesus in time and history gives us assurance no matter what age of history we might live in. Not only is Jesus present in our world—history is the arena in which He works in our behalf.

Revelation portrays Jesus working in human history through graphic imagery: He is now supervising His churches (Rev. 2:1-3:21); now controlling the course of history (Rev. 6:1-8:1); now calling a world to repentance (Rev. 8:3-11:13); now holding (will hold) our world morally accountable (Rev. 15:1-20:15); now establishing His reign on earth (Rev. 5:1-11:19). He will come to redeem His people (Rev. 14:14-20; 19:11-21) and will create new heavens and a new earth (Rev. 21:1-22:6). Not only has He died (Rev. 1:5; 5:6, 12; 12:10), but He has vanquished the enemy in both heaven and at the cross (Rev. 12:7-12). And He will fully complete His victory in the end. Such things are actual. Literal. Real. Historical. Not allegorical or metaphorical or symbolic. Interestingly, as the seals and trumpets suggest, the unfolding of the gospel in human history has been real, and the effects have been just as real.[16] People have been making real choices in history and subsequently determining the future course of history. Revelation assures us that Jesus is not isolated or apart from these realities. /

Most of us are familiar with the four different interpretive views of the book of Revelation: everything is past (preterist school); everything is future (futurist school); everything is just symbolic (idealist); or everything is rooted in history, either past, present, or future (historical school). Some prefer an eclectic approach that blends a little bit of each rather than staying with just one approach. Too many have forced Revelation's diverse perspectives into just one philosophical box. Actually, an eclectic approach is tacitly historicist in that it allows for the past and future while finding meaning for the present. However, it sends mixed signals about the nonbiblical presuppositions of other approaches and unwittingly undermines the unity of the book of Revelation—seeing it in parts rather than a seamless whole with a unified vision of God and His work through history, the human predicament, etc. A biblical historicism on the other hand affirms time and history as the sphere in which human beings live and make moral/spiritual choices. They are the arenas of God's activity in human affairs. Biblical historicism unfolds the scriptural perspective of covenant history in accordance with Revelation's (and Daniel's) cosmic controversy. Thus historical fulfillments are determined by their Christ-centeredness in accordance with the biblical perspective of history rather than forcing prophecy to fit the evening news. Biblical historicism is consistent with real life because it shows the work of God in the past, present, and future. It upholds the essential unity of Revelation's unveiling of Jesus with its vision of God's handling of evil.

As we have entered the third millennium, we find ourselves on the far horizon of the prophetic series. In addition to the preterist, futurists, and idealist interpretations, a prophetic interpretation—one that we may check against actual events in history—is ever more relevant.[17] No matter the actual events of history, however, Revelation affirms that Jesus is at work in history, controlling it, and moving it toward a certain glorious goal.

This is the view I need. So many things have happened in my world and in my life—and are still occurring right now around me—that I need to know whether Jesus really is here and whether He really cares. Are the natural disasters and geopolitical conflicts ranging around me simply that—natural and political? Or is there something sinister lurking in the background that's taking our hurting world toward a collision with eternity? Most of all, is Jesus aware of what's going on? Is He in control? Or do I have to create my own history?

The Bible consistently pulls the invisible and visible world together, connecting them in a wholistic way. It presents history in parallel scenes, with the invisible world operating behind the scenes. Occasionally the curtain lifts for a brief glimpse of God at work, but mainly Scripture keeps the focus on the visible world. God works through matter, through people, and through the events of history.[18] As Ellen White assures: "In the annals of human history the growth of nations, the rise and fall of empires, appear as dependent on the will and prowess of man. The shaping of events seems, to a great degree, to be determined by his power, ambition, or caprice. But in the Word of God the curtain is drawn aside, and we behold, behind, above, and through all the play and counterplay of human interests and power and passions, the agencies of the all-merciful One, silently, patiently working out the counsels of His own will.

"The Bible reveals the true philosophy of history."[19]

This is what the Apocalypse does. It shows us Jesus at work in every aspect of reality.

Tracing His Love

While all this points to the reality that Jesus is active in my existence, I cannot help wondering, *Where is He active in my life?* That's the question every one of us ponders and which the book of Revelation piques. And how can I know for sure?

The Lichtenwalter clan had a family reunion at Cedar Run Inn, a historic nineteenth-century railway station hotel with a full porch located in Cedar Run, Pennsylvania. It's a picturesque country place filled with antiques and quaint guest rooms that reflect a bygone era. I was sitting in the large room one evening with my mother. We were sipping hot drinks and flipping through some books filled with computer-generated 3-D art—the ones with colorful patterns filling the page, but bearing no apparent image.

"Do you see it?" she'd ask, pointing to another page of what seemed like random colors, as if the artist just went crazy spilling paint here and there.

"No, all I see is the patterns and colors."

"Look behind the surface . . . try to focus beyond . . ."

"No. Well . . . almost . . . ahhh. Oh! Yeaaaah! There it is . . ."

With such 3-D art one needs to remember that a three-dimensional image lurks within the otherwise random patterns and colors. The eyes must refocus as if what you are searching for is several inches behind the seemingly random colors. As you refocus a few inches "beyond" the page you let your mind capture patterns and colors to create what is there all the time—behind the obvious, the seen. It's incredible when your brain finally captures the three-dimensional images and they begin to emerge before your eyes. Some of them are very exciting to see. The whole process can be fun.

It reminds me of the world that Revelation portrays. When I read the book and I ponder the history it supposedly traverses, it doesn't always make sense. Too often it appears as just random visions and numbers and colorful imagery that doesn't seem to have any rhyme or reason except for a few terse pronouncements and promises here and there that more or less make sense. We are promised, though, that some profound truths lie deep within this literary masterpiece. In order to see what Revelation really wants me to find, I must focus beyond the surface and watch for the shapes of deep realities not accessible to the casual observer. This takes time. It means reading and rereading the book through prayerful study and persistently asking God to help me make those important connections so that I can see what He wants me to discover about His Son Jesus Christ.

Most of us Christians spend much of every day with eyes and minds focused on the surface of things—details about deadlines, delays, dollars, dress, food and shelter, going and coming, work and recreation, politics and more. Like the people in Lisbon, we drive right by *Christo Rei* and hardly notice or think anything about Jesus being present in our world. Attending to everyday issues is necessary and right, but our hearts must yearn to see the big picture, the cosmic meaning that lies behind the details. We must yearn for a sense of the presence of Jesus in our everyday happenings. The revelation shown to John unveils this deep pattern of Jesus ever present beneath the surface of history. How appropriate that before all else John sees the One who makes sense of time and history on a grand scale.[20]

I need to do that in my personal life as well. I must search for Jesus at work in my world and my life, tracing His presence in the historical events of my personal experience. Ellen White tells us that "among the cliffs and rocks of Patmos, John held communion with his Maker. He reviewed his past life, and at the thought of the blessings he had received, peace filled his heart."[21] As he did so, Jesus literally drew close and revealed Himself as present in John's world. The disciple consciously traced the presence of

Jesus throughout his life. Sixty years had gone by since Christ's crucifixion, but He had been there all the time. Now he suddenly became more clear to John than ever.

Psalm 107:43 declares: "Those who are wise will take all this to heart; they will see in our history the faithful love of the Lord" (NLT). That's what I want to do. I want to see in my own history the faithful love of Jesus. My study of the book of Revelation has certainly taught me one thing: the connection between Jesus and me is close and decided.[22]

In his whimsical autobiography the cartoonist James Thurber tells of flunking a college course in botany. Other students peered through their microscopes and drew the cellular structure of plants. Meanwhile Thurber, who suffered from an eye disorder, would protest, "I can't see anything." Each time it happened, the professor would at first respond patiently, making fine adjustments to the microscope, and then end in a fury when Thurber still could not see. A year later, attempting the class again, Thurber finally detected something worth drawing. He excitedly sketched the series of specks, dots, and patterns he saw in the eyepiece. The professor approached him with a broad smile, only to squint into the microscope and lose his temper once again. "That's your eye!" he shouted. "You've fixed the microscope so that it reflects! You've drawn your eye!"

I don't want to fix the lens of my reading of Revelation so that I view my own eye or my own agenda. Rather, I want to see Jesus. Revelation is a book that tells me what He has done, is doing, and will do for me.

I love Jesus because He is busy in my world. He is at work in my existence. Because He is, I am never alone and need never fear.

Is Jesus busy in your world? If so, what is He doing—right now, for you?

History is the arena in which Jesus is at work. That includes my own little world, my own short history. It's the only way that the apocalyptic gets personal.

---

[1] Ellen G. White, *Acts of the Apostles,* p. 581.

[2] Johnson, *The Triumph of the Lamb,* p. 55.

[3] Richard Bauckham, *The Theology of the Book of Revelation* (Cambridge, Eng.: Cambridge University Press, 1993), p. 12.

[4] Bauckham, pp. 12-17; Osborne, *Revelation,* pp. 12, 13; David E. Aune, *Revelation 1-5* (Dallas: Word Books, 1997), pp. lxxii-lxxiii.

[5] David W. Hall, *The Millennium of Jesus Christ: An Exposition of the Revelation for All*

Ages (Oak Ridge, Tenn.: The Calvin Institute, 1998), p. 41.

[6] Ellen G. White, *Testimonies for Ministers,* p. 114.

[7] Henry and Richard Blackaby, *Spiritual Leadership: Moving People on to God's Agenda* (Nashville: Broadman and Holman, 2001), p. 201.

[8] Stefanovic, *Revelation of Jesus Christ,* pp. 98, 103; Thomas, *Revelation 1-7: An Exegetical Commentary* (Chicago: Moody Press, 1992), p. 115.

[9] Osborne, p. 97.

[10] Beale, *The Book of Revelation,* pp. 152-159.

[11] Craig S. Keener, *Revelation: The NIV Application Commentary* (Grand Rapids: Zondervan, 2000), p. 98.

[12] Easley, *Revelation,* p. 20.

[13] Ellen White reminds us that Revelation's truths "are addressed to those living in the last days of this earth's history, as well as to those living in the days of John. Some of the scenes depicted in this prophecy are in the past, some are now taking place; some bring to view the close of the great conflict between the powers of darkness and the Prince of heaven, and some reveal the triumphs and joys of the redeemed in the earth made new" (Ellen G. White, *Acts of the Apostles,* p. 584).

[14] Humphrey, "A Tale of Two Cities and (At Least) Three Women," pp. 81, 82.

[15] Hans K. LaRondelle, "The Heart of Historicism," *Ministry* (Sept. 2005), pp. 22-27.

[16] Stefanovic, pp. 218, 223; Stott, *The Incomparable Christ,* pp. 187-197.

[17] Doukhan, *Secrets of Revelation,* p. 29.

[18] Philip Yancey, *Rumors of Another World: What on Earth Are We Missing?* (Grand Rapids: Zondervan, 2003), p. 184.

[19] Ellen G. White, *Education,* p. 173.

[20] Johnson, p. 50.

[21] Ellen G. White, *Acts of the Apostles,* p. 571.

[22] Ellen G. White, *Testimonies to Ministers,* p. 114.

CHAPTER 5

I LOVE
JESUS BECAUSE . . .

HE TALKS TO ME

In the Blink of an Ear
Revelation 2:1, 8, 12, 18; 3:1, 7, 14, 22

He bemused the West with his litany of claimed victories over its coalition troops, and amused Arabs with his bottomless dictionary of insults. Standing in front of the cameras, a grim smile on his face and a military beret on his head, he would declare forcefully in fluent English and Arabic, "There are no American troops in Baghdad!" Meanwhile, black smoke rose in the distance behind him, weapons fire rattled all around, and U.S. tanks rumbled down streets only yards away. Day after day he would seek the foreign news media and burst forth with original and very colorful words to describe the intensifying crisis, dispute coalition advances, and spew out anti-American and anti-British invectives.

In an age of spin Iraq's information minister Mohammed Saeed al-Sahhaf offered feeling and authenticity. His message was consistent—unshakable, in fact, no matter the evidence—but he commanded daily attention by his on-the-spot, invective-rich variations on the theme. It didn't matter that he was so wildly off the mark about the state of the conflict. News broadcasts would split the television screen with Sahhaf on one side claiming there were no coalition forces in Baghdad and show on the other side U.S. tanks driving down the street. The emotional power of his telecast appearances counted far more than their accuracy.

"He makes everyone feel good even if we know it's all lies," one Arab journalist wrote. No matter what he said, Sahhaf was defending Iraqi honor, playing the psychological war game in which words create reality.

Such classic moments in the Iraqi "war of words" reveal an insatiable human desire to hear something—anything!—when one's world is threatened and uncertainty hangs in the air. It is especially true in time of war, when information is crucial and the outcome affects one's very life or future. Times of upheaval remind us how limited we are, making us feel vulnerable, inadequate, powerless, and often hopeless. During such moments people seek perspective, hope, and information so that they can be assured and make good decisions. So they long for information. Even if they know that it may be just lies, they will listen to anything just to keep their fragmenting world together—at least their inner world. Sometimes things can be extremely confusing because the voices seem different from what one actually sees or experiences. Or they conflict not only with what one experiences but with one another as well.

When I'm discouraged or worried, I crave words of encouragement. During those times I am doing well, I long for affirmation. And the times I am straying, I need someone to warn and guide me. Whether it is a formal letter, a phone call, a brief comment, a little note, an e-mail or voice mail, it doesn't matter, only that someone is connecting to me where I am. So when someone speaks, it resonates one way or another.

Most of all, I need a clear and trusted voice. Perhaps you remember the anxious moments as the first hours of the Iraqi war unfolded. Almost everyone was glued to their TV or radio. Wherever you were in the world, you wanted to hear something. Incredibly, Sahhaf's words made people feel good even if they that knew it was all lies.

By the time he abruptly disappeared from public view he had become a media star and heroic defender of Iraqi honor, earning even the admiration of those who had written him off as "a lot of hot air." People really loved watching Sahhaf speak, regardless of what he was saying. A Web site emerged both to honor and to poke admiring fun at his dogged defense of Saddam's regime and his skewering of opponents.

Never Quiet

Revelation introduces Jesus as speaking. His voice is like the arresting, piercing sound of a trumpet that cannot be ignored (Rev. 1:10; 4:1) or rushing waters crashing against rocks (Rev. 1:15). On Patmos John likely would have had a hard time getting away from the insistent noise of the breakers pounding the island's coast. To put it another way, the voice of Jesus is the Word of God that must be constantly heard and obeyed.[1]

Then we have the two-edged sword coming out of Christ's mouth (verse 16). The sword demonstrates what takes place when Jesus speaks.[2] Words challenge (Rev. 2:16), conquer (Rev. 19:15), and create reality. By changing thinking and lives, they can produce courage, hope, perspective, and peace. And words can cut both ways by either killing or bringing life (Rev. 6:4; 19:21). The double-edged sword in His mouth offers salvation for the believer but destruction for the unbelievers. The book of Hebrews tells us that "the word of God is full of living power. It is sharper than the sharpest knife, cutting deep into our innermost thoughts and desires. It exposes us for what we really are. Nothing in all creation can hide from him. Everything is naked and exposed before his eyes. This is the God to whom we must explain all that we have done" (Heb. 4:12, 13, NLT). Scripture links the Word with Jesus as if they are one. He is the Word of God (Rev. 19:13; cf. John 1:1-14).

Interestingly, the book of Revelation arranges the seven items used to describe the Son of man symmetrically. It links the first and last items (the white head and shining face) (Rev. 1:14, 16), the second and sixth items (eyes and mouth) (verses 14, 16), and the third and fifth items (feet and right hand) as paired members of the body (verses 15, 16). The fourth item in the series of seven is the voice of Jesus (verse 16). It is at the center.[3] All images of Revelation converge in this voice that thunders of passionate love and urgent mercy.

Thus Jesus speaks to His church. We see Him walking among His gathered, listening, praying, believing, struggling, hurting, and troubled people. One phrase repeats without variation in the messages to the seven churches: ta,de le,gei (*táide légei*), i.e., "says this" (Rev. 2:1, 8, 12, 18; 3:1, 7, 14). Jesus stands in the middle of His church speaking. That's important to notice, because the seven churches were having problems. Their world was falling apart as they faced real enemies, trials, fear, and loss. Some wondered what to think, what to do. How long would it all last? How much would they have to endure? They needed Jesus to say something to them. The vision of the seven churches isn't simply telling us that He has an agenda, so "Listen up!" Rather it's a picture of a church consisting of individual Christians in a lost world in need of an unmistakable "Word from the Lord."

Never silent, Jesus stands in the midst of His church and speaks. But in contrast to Iraq's information minister, He is "the faithful and true witness" who ever tells the truth (Rev. 3:14; 19:11; cf. Rev. 3:7; 6:10; 19:9; 21:5; 22:6). Jesus presents it as it really is. Nor will He suddenly disappear when the going gets rough. Furthermore, His Word is as good as His voice.

Another phrase that appears without variation to the seven churches is: "He who has an ear, let him hear what the Spirit says to the churches" (Rev. 2:7, 11, 17, 29; 3:6, 13, 22, NKJV). The last word spoken to every church by the Great Senior Pastor who walks among His people is the command to "hear what the Spirit says to the churches." In other words, when Jesus speaks, so does the Spirit. Whatever differences might exist among the seven churches, Jesus maintains two things as constant: the Spirit ultimately declares what Jesus says, and the people are to listen.[4]

We find yet another recurring phase that we need to add to the link between Jesus and the Spirit speaking. Each letter to the churches begins with: "Unto the angel of the church in [wherever] write." Put it in a book (Rev. 1:11). What Jesus says is not only able to be literally spoken and heard, but also written down, read, and kept (Rev. 1:3, 11; 14:13; 19:9; 21:5; 22:6, 9, 18, 19). That assumes that what Jesus has to say has understandable form, content, and, most vital, meaning (Rev. 1:3; 22:9). While truth in the Apocalypse is a Person, it also has to do with ideas and words that are concrete, objective, and propositional.[5] This is important in our postmodern age in which words supposedly don't mesh with reality.

Let's look at our extended link. Jesus communicates through His Spirit via the written Word (the book of Revelation) that the Spirit has inspired. Jesus speaks through the Spirit, who inspires John to write words in a book that we read (the book of Revelation) and through which the Spirit speaks to us. Christ is in the midst of His church speaking, and He does so by the Word (Revelation) that He has inspired through the Holy Spirit. A close link exists between Jesus and the Spirit, between Jesus and the Word, and between the Spirit and the words of the book of Revelation. The power is in the Word, not the prophet who conveys those words. Listening ears means being attentive to Spirit-spoken words—Scripture (in this case the book of Revelation). The Word of Jesus is as good as the voice of Jesus. The Spirit mediates the meaning of the Word to our hearts (by way of understanding, conviction, and invitation).

Consider one more aspect of the imagery of Jesus standing in the midst of His church speaking. The book of Revelation assumes that a reciter stands before the community in the place of John, who is himself confined to Patmos (Rev. 1:3, 9). "Blessed is he who reads," John asserts (verse 3, NKJV). In hearing the voice of the reciter, the seven churches in effect listen to that of their exiled pastor, John, which ultimately is the voice of Jesus speaking through him to them (Rev. 1:1, 2, 11, 19; 22:8, 16). The public reader actually acts as the voice of Jesus.[6] John heard and saw and wrote (Rev. 22:8). Then the public readers simply recite what is written. In the process, they make Jesus present in the community.[7] In this way He continues to speak in the Apocalypse, regardless of how much longer John may have lived or the seven geographically located churches continued to survive. Even today He still stands in the midst of His church speaking!

Says This . . .

When our world is threatened and uncertainty hangs in the air, we need a word from the Lord. But what would He tell us? What we hear Jesus saying to the seven churches gives us a glimpse of the different kinds of things that He would tell us today as we experience similar situations. We have already learned that the whole book of Revelation is a circular letter written to seven specific churches: Ephesus, Smyrna, Pergamum, Thyatira, Sardis, Philadelphia, and Laodicea (Rev. 1:4, 11; 22:16). We have discovered, too, that many misreadings have resulted from neglecting this simple fact—it is as much (if not more) a letter as it is apocalyptic prophecy.[8]

But while the book locates the seven churches geographically, it defines them theologically.[9] Christ's seven messages show us that the seven churches were each quite different, facing unique problems and reacting very differently to common problems (Rev. 2:1-3:21). But while He speaks individually to each church, the messages are not self-contained. Each is an introduction to the rest of the book.[10] In other words, we should read Revelation from seven explicit perspectives.[11] The varied perspectives are articulated within a broader common situation that all seven churches share. This enables John to engage seven different spiritual/moral contexts in which the Apocalypse would be read and also to integrate those contexts into the broader perspective of the book,[12] i.e., the tyranny of Rome, the cosmic conflict of God and evil, the eschatological purpose of God for His whole creation, and the life and morality consistent with faith in the Lamb. In this way John shows the Christians of each of the seven churches how the dilemmas of their local context belong to, and must be understood in light of, larger spiritual/moral issues.[13] Revelation's prophetic message is thus explicitly and carefully contextualized in seven specific backgrounds.

In the process Jesus reveals many things about our world, our church, the situation we live in, and even something about ourselves—all from a heavenly perspective. Beyond that, He tells us something about Himself.

78

This section of the book of Revelation teaches us about hope and how to live in the world as we wait for His return. We hear promise and exhortation.

To Ephesus, who had lost its love for Jesus, He seems to be saying, "Look at Me! I hold you in My hand—you belong to Me and are accountable to Me. Just as I have not lost My first love for you, keep your love for Me. A paradise with a tree of life awaits you" (see Rev. 2:1-7).

To the suffering church at Smyrna we hear Him declaring that He knows what's happening in our lives as we choose to be faithful to Him. The challenges, the trials, the opposition, the suffering, the sacrifices—He understands them all. The faithful will receive a crown of life that negates the second death (see verses 8-11).

To His people living in Pergamum Jesus acknowledges how difficult it is to live in certain places in the world where the devil and all evil seem so "in your face" and truth gets fuzzy. He is fully aware how the world and its values can be so overwhelming and bewitching that we feel intimidated to the point that it becomes easy to compromise in those seemingly unimportant lifestyle matters. We hear him tell how we can be publicly faithful but privately flawed. How He's concerned that our compromise with the world dulls the effectiveness of our witness, but that He still holds out to us a rich promise of spiritual nourishment and a special intimate relationship with Him (see verses 12-17).

To the compromising at Thyatira Jesus reminds us how we can run smack into some Jezebel who's overpowering the church with her charismatic leadership and compromising agenda. How we can be so deluded by our feelings of insignificance that we can easily follow questionable leadership. And how while His faithful may always be a remnant, His incredible promises will enable them to be an unstoppable moral power no matter what. When we hold on to what we have and keep His deeds until the end, we'll see the face of the Morning Star (see verses 18-29; Rev. 22:16).

To the spiritually dead at Sardis He asserts that some congregations are merely a morgue with a steeple—outwardly alive, but spiritually dead inside. Some, though, can remain very much alive and not soil their character garments. Jesus promises that they will walk with Him dressed in white. It is enough to wake up the dead among us if we but have ears to hear. And those who do so will never have their names erased from the book of life (see Rev. 3:1-6).

To the tiny congregation in Philadelphia Jesus promises an astounding opportunity and incredible guarantees. It is not surprising that, at the threshold of its open doors, there stands a cross—of unbelievable pressures and difficulties. In the midst of their inadequacies and hounding difficulties they had to decide whether to give up, give in, or go on. Would they make their suffering a wall or a door? Wonderful blessings come to those who overcome—access to God, character that mirrors the Father and Jesus, and the ethics of the Holy City (see verses 7-13).

And finally to those who lost their spiritual passion in Laodicea, we hear Jesus asking whether we are lukewarm or hot. Halfhearted or whole-hearted. Passionless or passionate for God. That's the question Christ's visit to Laodicea raises. Neither cold nor hot, thinking they lacked nothing, they had a pretty good opinion of themselves. But Jesus shook them up with both some sharp criticism and some incredible promises. Will it be enough to fire our passion for God? It depends on what we really want to hear and believe about ourselves—and of the Jesus who tells it like it is. Will we invite Him into our hearts and choose to overcome as He over-came (see verses 14-22)?

Jesus has so much to say to the churches, both those of the first cen-tury and of every age. Thoughts of love, suffering, truth, holiness, sincer-ity, mission, and wholeheartedness fill His mind.[14] He warns us how the world tries to squeeze the church into its mold or crush it. That tribulation and persecution threaten it from outside and that sins developing out of a life of faith itself seek to destroy from within. We need affirmation, we need correction, and we need motivation.

So Jesus speaks. He talks not only to a busy world but also to me. That's why I love Him!

Do I Really Need to Hear This?

What did you think of my chapter title—"In the Blink of an Ear"? Sounds strange, doesn't it? Eyes blink but not ears, right?

But it's a fact! Our middle ear has three interconnected bones (the malleus, incus, and stapes) that transfer sound energy from the eardrum to the fluid-filled inner ear. When a sudden loud noise occurs, muscles holding the three bones immediately tighten through an "acoustic re-flex," reducing by a factor of up to 100 the amount of energy reaching the inner ear. Just as eyelids blink, so this reflex gives the ear a way to protect itself.[15] Military gunners understand this principle and often have a loud click sound (or smaller explosion detonate) before the big guns go off.

We may have ears to hear, but sometimes we immediately tighten them against some of the hard or uncomfortable sayings of Jesus. Such sayings create an "acoustic reflex" to His criticism, warning, advice, or invitation.

I haven't always heard everything that's been said to me. And neither have you! We don't always hear, even when we have two perfectly good ears. Human beings have a tremendous capacity to filter out or tune into things, depending on our interest. Thus we hear what we want to hear and all too often don't hear some things at all.

This became plain to me while I was in the Ukraine holding an evangelistic crusade. I'd often find the Ukrainian family I lived with talking up a storm. But because I didn't know the language and my translator wasn't taking the time to include me in the conversation, it was all a bunch of meaningless noise to me. And so I would drift off into my own thoughts. No longer consciously aware of what was going on around me, I would literally not hear the voices or sounds. I had completely tuned them out.

After that happened a couple times, I realized that I didn't have to be in the Ukraine to ignore the sounds of life around me. I can be absorbed in thought so completely that I am totally oblivious of life (and people) around me. I can sit at my own table at home and do it. As I sit there eating and thinking, my wife, Kathie, across the table talking away, will suddenly wave her hand in front of may face, saying with a bit of frustration, "Hello! Hello! Anybody there?" First I notice the wildly waving hand. Next I see the unhappy face. And then it takes conscious effort to shake myself loose from whatever has absorbed my mind and get back in touch with what is being said to me or is happening around me. When I shared this one time with a woman I was talking to, she shot back with a wild expression in her eyes, "That's just what my husband does. It's frustrating to no end to say something to him and there's no response whatsoever. It's as if he's deaf." An old adage claims that many men are indeed deaf at the sound frequency levels which their wives speak.

Of course, parents make the same comment about their children. Any of us can be so absorbed in something that we miss a class assignment, or somebody's cry for help, or the voice of our own children. We can hear what we want to hear and filter out what we don't (selective attention). Or we can "focus" our ear on a target, filtering frequencies to help us zero in on a single voice across the room. And we can become oblivious to sounds that we've heard a thousand times. Thus when others speak, our minds wander. When we disagree with somebody, we shut the person out of our attention. We can even hear things never said, or remember only part of what was actually spoken.

Return with me to one of those three phrases repeated without variation in the messages to the seven churches of Revelation: "He who has an ear, let him hear what the Spirit says to the churches" (Rev. 2:7, 11, 17, 29; 3:6, 13, 22, NKJV). Whatever the differences among the churches, two things are constant: the Spirit speaks, and the people are to listen.[16] Listening ears means being attentive to Spirit-spoken words.

Revelation thus places emphasis on the primacy of hearing, and raises the question of its quality. Listening is a spiritual act far more than an acoustical function. Revelation calls us to a personal act of listening. The church is the one place in the world in which people deliberately come together and uncover their ears so that the sounds of God's Word will be heard accurately and believingly.[17] The church is not a building or an institution or a place, but people gathered together to hear Jesus speak. Listening is the church's common task.[18] There can be no church apart from listening to the Christ who stands in its midst speaking.[19]

John informs me that Jesus still stands in the center of His church speaking—not to everyone in general, but to me, personally (note Revelation's distinction between the "one who has an ear" and what is said "to the churches"). But do I hear Him speaking? That depends on whether I sense my need for a word from my apocalyptic Pastor. If I love Jesus, I will be glad that He has something to tell me about the time and place and circumstances of my life, the church, and the world. And if I need His voice ringing in my ear, I will love Him because He is there already speaking—affirming, correcting, motivating.

That's why I love Jesus. Constantly talking to me, He has something to say about everything going on in my life and my world and my church. I want to be sensitive to His voice, welcoming His counsel, accepting His evaluation, heeding His warnings, responding to His reproofs, and rejoicing in His grace and promises. How better could I respond to His love than to hear and heed and hope?

---

[1] Easley, *Revelation*, p. 19.

[2] Peterson, *Reversed Thunder*, p. 37.

[3] *Ibid.*, pp. 38, 39.

[4] *Ibid.*, p. 47.

[5] We need to be careful in defining "prepositional." Here we understand that it means biblical revelation has cognitive content, that it informs us about revelatory events and their

meaning. See Arthur F. Holmes, *All Truth Is God's Truth* (Downers Grove, Ill.: InterVarsity Press, 1983), p. 74.

[6] David L. Barr, "The Apocalypse of John as Oral Enactment," *Interpretation,* vol. 40, no. 3 (July 1986), p. 251.

[7] *Ibid.,* p. 252.

[8] Bauckham, *The Theology of the Book of Revelation,* p. 12.

[9] Peterson, p. 46.

[10] Bauckham, p. 14.

[11] *Ibid.*

[12] Aune, *Revelation 1-5,* pp. lxxii–lxxiii.

[13] Bauckham, p. 15; Osborne, pp. 12, 13.

[14] Stott, *The Incomparable Christ,* pp. 178–181.

[15] Lowell Ponte, "In the Blink of an Ear," *Reader's Digest,* Oct. 1993, p. 110.

[16] Peterson, p. 47.

[17] *Ibid.,* p. 49.

[18] *Ibid.*

[19] *Ibid.,* p. 48.

CHAPTER 6

I LOVE JESUS BECAUSE . . .

HE KNOWS EVERYTHING ABOUT ME

When There Aren't Enough Rocks to Throw
Revelation 2:8-10

The movie *Forrest Gump* contains a heart-wrenching scene in which 5-year-old Jenny, Forrest's friend, prays as the two of them run into a cornfield to hide from her drunken father: "Dear God, make me a bird so I can fly far, far away from here." Her father has been sexually abusing her, and although the next day he was arrested and Jenny went to live with someone else, her struggles over what he did to her had only begun. In fact, she spends the rest of her life trying to recover from the damage.

Years later Jenny returns to the small town of her childhood to visit Forrest. The two of them, now adults in their 30s, are walking near the abandoned shack where she once lived. As she fixes her eyes on it, painful buried memories of the abuse flood her mind. Bursting into tears, she begins to vent her hurt and anger by picking up the rocks around her and throwing them as hard as she can at the shack. When there are no more rocks, she takes off her shoes and throws them too. Finally she falls on the ground, sobbing.

As Forrest reflects on the scene, he says, "Sometimes I guess there just aren't enough rocks."

When you think about the pain in your life, do you find yourself resonating with Forrest's observation? Perhaps you have been verbally, physically, or sexually abused. Maybe you've experienced the wrenching pain of a divorce, grew up in a chaotic home with an alcoholic parent, or lost a loved one in a senseless accident. Have you been deeply hurt in a relationship or felt the aching loneliness of abandonment or ostracism? Or could it be that a work situation treated you unfairly or church or family members or a friend or spouse betrayed you? Like Jenny, you could throw a few rocks—knowing deep inside there will never be enough of them to throw, because the hurt seems so unbearable. Not only are there not enough stones for what you have already experienced, but like Jenny, you long to be a bird so that you can fly far away from what you may be experiencing right now. You can't help wondering, *Why is this happening to me?* And so you think and burst out, "God, it isn't fair." Or you may ask yourself, "Does God hear? Does He know? Does He even care?"

The Smyrnaean church was filled with deeply hurting people who faced poverty, ridicule, abuse, persecution, imprisonment, suffering, and death. As victims of mob violence, vandalism, and looting, they were hard pressed to keep their jobs, their homes, and their possessions.[1] Tongues wagged busily all around them, and false rumors circulated constantly, poisoning the public against them. It was painful to be misunderstood, caricatured, and boycotted.[2] While their trials seemed endless, worse was yet to come: prison and death.

Smyrna (modern Izmir, Turkey) was one of the hardest places in Asia to be a Christian. No believers faced a more uncertain future than in this ancient city. A small church, they had few economic resources as they faced a hostile world. No doubt individuals within that congregation often wished they could be a little bird so they could "fly far, far away from here." As hurting human beings, with feelings and emotions like every one of us, it would be only natural to want to throw a few stones at some of those who personally hurt them, or at life in general.

Easily reading right past such things when we study the book of Revelation, we usually don't connect on the emotional and psychological level those verses hint at. We read for theology, for doctrine, for facts so we can properly place Smyrna (and the rest of the churches) in their place in history. In the process we forget that these churches consisted of real people with faces, names, feelings, emotions, fears, needs, and longings. The life of faith always and necessarily takes place in a community of persons located somewhere in time and place. If we would connect concretely with Revelation's personal concerns we must keep in mind that they involved real people.

The city of Smyrna has at least one face for us to imagine. One of the best-known Christian martyrs of all ages was a native of this ancient city.

Revelation's Great Love Story

Bishop Polycarp was in all probability already a member of the church there when John wrote out Christ's message to this hurting congregation. Tradition implies that he may have even met John personally. Whatever the case, Polycarp would have read John's letter to the Smyrnaean Christians and no doubt pondered its message. Perhaps it was a source of strength to him when his own hour of trial came.

It occurred in the year 156. Polycarp had fled Smyrna at the concerned appeals of his congregation. But when the authorities tracked him down to his hiding place, he made no attempt to run farther. Instead, he offered food and drink to his captors and asked permission to retire for prayer. Two hours later he got up from his knees and they took him away. As they approached Smyrna, the officer in charge urged Polycarp to recant. "What harm can it do," he asked, "to sacrifice to the emperor?" But Polycarp refused. When they arrived in the city, his captors pushed him out of the carriage they had transported him in and brought him before the proconsul in the local amphitheater.

"Have you any respect to your old age," the proconsul asked, "then swear by the genius of Caesar. Swear, and I will release you. Revile Christ."

"Eighty-six years I've served Him," Polycarp answered firmly. "And He has done me no wrong. How can I blaspheme my King, who saved me?"

"Swear by the genius of Caesar," the proconsul persisted. "I have wild beasts. If you will not change your mind, I will throw you to them."

"Bid them to be brought!"

"As you despise the beasts, unless you change your mind I'll burn you with fire."

"You threaten me with fire that burns for a season, and after a little while it goes out; for you are ignorant of the fire of the judgment to come, and of everlasting punishment reserved for the ungodly. But what are you waiting for? Bring what you will."

The more Polycarp spoke, the more he was filled with courage and joy. Some say his face grew full of grace and peace.

"Polycarp has confessed himself to be a Christian," the amazed proconsul proclaimed.

An infuriated mob gathered wood for the pyre. "This is the teacher of Asia, the father of the Christians, the destroyer of our gods, the man who teaches many not to sacrifice or even to worship," it shouted.

Soon Polycarp stood by the stake. "He who has given me power to abide the fire will enable me to abide untroubled at the flames," he said. Then he prayed: "O Lord, Almighty God, the Father of Your beloved Son Jesus Christ, through whom we have received a knowledge of You . . . I thank You that You have thought me worthy, this day and this hour, to share the cup of Your Christ among the number of Your witnesses!"

When the mob kindled the fire, a great flame flashed out. But then a wind kept driving the flames away, prolonging his agony. A soldier finally drew his sword and put an end to Polycarp's misery.[3]

The letter to the church of Smyrna is especially for those going through real life with its hard times.[4] We can apply it on two levels. First it speaks of persecution and suffering endured for Christ (because of one's faith and the truth of the gospel and God's Word). Then we have its theological underpinning in which it alludes to more general trials, abuse, and suffering—ones that may be not particularly linked to our faith journey, but that become a focal point of the strength of our relationship with Jesus.[5] Hudson Taylor put it well when he spoke of how life's trials can bring us either closer to Christ or push us away from Him. It depends on where they are located in our thinking and experience. If the trials come between ourselves and Christ, they will inevitably divide us from Him. But if Christ is on one side and our trials on the other, the trials will push us closer to Him. Every moment of suffering ultimately brings us to the question of our relationship with Christ.

Revelation acknowledges the pain and wickedness that lurk everywhere in our world when it exhorts us to endure and persevere (Rev. 1:9; 2:2, 3; 3:10; 13:10; 14:12). Otherwise, why would one need to endure or persevere if there were no trials, pressures, or sorrows? The book also promises that one day God will gently wipe away every tear from our eyes: "He will remove all of their sorrows, and there will be no more death or sorrow or crying or pain. For the old world and its evils are gone forever" (Rev. 21:4, NLT; cf. Rev. 7:17; 21:4; Isa. 25:8; 35:10; 65:19). The context suggests that God accounts for the wounds of the past—that He will heal the pain of our past history.[6]

At the opening of the fifth seal we hear innocent people pleading, "How long, O Lord" (Rev. 6:10). They have lost everything dear to them, including their lives. So they cry out! They want to throw a few stones—or at least have God stand up in their behalf and avenge them. While the context is the faithful people of God who suffered unjustly for their faith during the tribulation of the Middle Ages, their haunting cry reflects the anguish of the innocent of all ages: "And in her was found the blood of prophets and

of saints and *of all who have been slain on the earth*" (Rev. 18:24, NASB).[7]
(Interestingly, the fifth trumpet also reflects incredible pain as people are so
filled with psychological suffering and terror that they plunge into dark despair to the point at which they long to die but death now eludes them [Rev.
9:6]. Thus we find the hurting righteous in the fifth seal and the hurting lost
in the fifth trumpet.) Wherever we turn in Revelation we hear the cries and
find images of suffering and hurting people.

Christians living in Smyrna no doubt suffered for Jesus, but their pain
and sorrow echo the cry of hurting, innocent hearts everywhere, through
all time. This letter fits our experience today.[8]

Never Alone . . .

In the previous two chapters we have learned that Jesus is busy in our
world and still stands at the center of His church speaking—not to
everyone in general, but to each of us, personally. That's why I love Jesus.
Never silent, He always has something to say about everything going on
in my life, my world, and my church. Oh, how I need His continuous
voice in my ear! But when the going gets tough and I'm hurting deep inside, yearning to fly like a bird or to throw a few stones, I want to know,
"Does Jesus hear *me? my* cry? Does He know and care what happens to me
personally?"

"Nobody knows the trouble I've seen," the old spiritual pines.
Sometimes we can feel incredibly alone in our pain. So misunderstood
and unheard—like a hole in the air. That's how my wife describes it
sometimes. In other words, a nothing, something insignificant, voiceless,
nameless, and unacknowledged.

"Who knows? Who cares? Who understands?" we ask ourselves.

So Jesus speaks. "I know," He says. "I know everything you've been
through. Everything you are experiencing right now." "I know your
tribulation and your poverty and the slander of those who profess to know
Me" (see Rev. 2:9). Then He adds, "Besides what you're experiencing
right now, I know what's on the horizon—what tomorrow will bring and
how it will not get any better. In addition to your present stress and abuse,
you will face imprisonment and death. Your suffering is about to get
worse. The tribulation will intensify to the point that some of you will be
put in prison and some of you will die violently" (see verse 10).

Jesus knows exactly what is (and will be) happening to us. His words
to the church at Pergamum reveal His awareness of their exact situation:
"I know where you live—right there in Satan's lair" (see verse 13). But I

wonder, *What does Jesus know? Just the facts? Or does He know how I feel? Is He aware of my inner emotional needs as I go through those struggles?* Think about it. What is Jesus really saying here and throughout the book of Revelation?

I believe that Jesus is assuring us: "I know your tribulation. I know how you have been treated—blasphemed, persecuted, imprisoned, killed. And I know your tears and how you feel—hurt, alone, frustrated, powerless, helpless, and angry. I know how hard it is to hang in there when you are getting tired and things only worsen. I know how you want to give up or lash out in anger or retaliation. I hear your questions of why and fairness. I hear your prayers. I really do know."

Here is the heart of Revelation's message to our hurting world. The connection between Christ and His people is close and decided.

"Nobody knows but Jesus," the spiritual goes on to avow. That's why I love Jesus. I love Him because He understands what I am going through right now. The trials I am facing. My questions and confusion. How I want to lash out, run, compromise, give up altogether—anything to stop the pain.

"Doom and Destruction?" the bold headline read. "While the book of Revelation can be a frightening peek into the future, a Seventh-day Adventist pastor maintains that it is really a book of hope and a pathway to inner peace," began the full-spread religion feature article (including color picture) about some lectures that I was about to share in my community: "Is There Hope in the Apocalypse?" Somehow one of the staff writers of our county paper got word of my 10-part series and called for an interview. Someone had told her how I had memorized the book and would bring a different spin to how most people read Scripture's last book. So I told her about the 10 heart-probing topics I would cover and the biblical images of Jesus that would bring hope, compel decision, and stir love. We talked candidly about some of Revelation's violent imagery and unrelenting strife and suffering, as well the fact that the book is about Jesus—not the antichrist or the mark of the beast or any number of other things that people usually associate with it. Her surprise was evident throughout, but no more than my own amazement at how she very professionally conveyed my focus to the reading audience. The caption under the 6" x 8" picture of me sitting at my desk with the book in hand couldn't have said it better: "Seventh-day Adventist pastor Larry Lichtenwalter insists that the Bible's book of Revelation is not about doom and destruction, but about Jesus and hope."

Revelation's Great Love Story

The most exciting moment in this unexpected interview occurred when a staff photographer came to my office for a shoot. He was a guy named Neal, clearly in his 20s, with gel-piked hair, pierced ear, chain hanging around his neck, and classy casual clothes—a typical postmodern young person in both look and mannerisms.

"Are you the one speaking on revolutions?" he asked with a questioning look. I immediately realized that he didn't know much about Scripture's last book, let alone the Bible as a whole. "Revolutions!"

That was a first for me. But it opened my heart. *Why, Lord, did I get this interview in the first place, and why this guy to shoot my picture?* After the usual formalities and small talk he asked me to sit at my desk with the book of Revelation open in my hands and talk, as if I were telling him about Revelation (he got it right that time). That was my cue. I realized that I would likely never have a shot at this guy again. Now was my time to pack the moment with Revelation's Jesus. So I said, "Neal, you know what I like about this book?"

"No," he replied as he started clicking.

"I like this book because it tells me about a Jesus who is busy in my world and knows everything there is about me. He knows where I live. He knows what I am doing. He knows about my sorrows and troubles and verbal abuse and slander, and . . ." Despite his constant turning this way and that as he concentrated on the composition of each shot, I knew he was listening. I watched increasing interest in his expression as I spoke of Jesus in Revelation. As I moved from verse to verse, telling more and more about a Jesus who cares and engenders hope, I silently prayed that the Holy Spirit would forever rivet these images in his mind as my own image was being etched on film.

Postmodern young people have a keen sense of our world's brokenness. Most of them know it firsthand. They struggle for identity, belonging, purpose, and meaning. Revelation's images of Jesus are powerful for a generation longing for hope, significance, and endurng relationships.

"I know your tribulation. I know where you live. I know what you are doing. I know everything about you. I know," Jesus says. "I know."

Everything I Need

But Revelation goes even deeper. To this little hurting congregation Jesus says, "First—before you know what I know—I want to tell something about Myself. I want you to know who I am." I am "the first and the last, who was dead and has come to life" (Rev. 2:8, NASB). "As the 'first and the last' I have power over time. I am the Lord of history. Nothing happens here apart from My knowledge. When it's all over, I will be standing there at the end welcoming you, helping you come through. Everything will finally be as I have promised. But most of all, I want you to know that I have personally experienced the full range of human suffering. You see, 'I was dead . . .' Remember? On the cross I suffered injustice. There I felt the shame of nakedness. I was deprived of My rights. I endured taunting. I, too, was the focus of other people's slander and rage. Rejected and forsaken, I endured excruciating pain, thirst, hunger, emptiness, torment, confusion, and finally, death itself. 'I was dead.' "

I like the pastoral way that theologian Frank Lake puts it: "Christ's own being on the cross contained all the clashing contrarieties and scandalous fates of human existence. Life Himself was identified with death; the Light of the world was enveloped in darkness. The feet of the Man who said 'I am the Way' feared to tread upon it and prayed, 'If it be possible, not that way.' The Water of Life was thirsty. The Bread of Life was hungry. The divine Lawgiver was Himself unjustly outlawed. The Holy One was identified with the unholy. The Lion of Judah was a crucified lamb. The hands that made the world and raised the dead were fixed by nails until they were rigid in death. Men's hope of heaven descended into hell."[9]

It means that Jesus can truly identify with us when we suffer, because He has personally experienced the breadth and depth of human suffering. The book of Hebrews tells us that Jesus "learned obedience from the things which he suffered" (Heb. 5:8, NASB) and was made "perfect through sufferings" (Heb. 2:10). Because He has been "touched with the feeling of our infirmities" (Heb. 4:15), He can empathetically identify with our distress, hurt, and sorrow.

"But," Jesus says in those three pregnant words: "who was dead," "I didn't just suffer personally on the cross. I suffered vicariously." Because I was "a man of sorrows and acquainted with grief," I also bore your griefs and carried your sorrows (Isa. 53:3, 4). Jesus endured not only His own suffering but, in some mysterious way, yours, mine, and that of the world as well.[10] There on the cross Jesus bore our sins. There, too, He bore our sufferings. We are both sinners and sufferers—villains and victims. The cross of Jesus touches both needs. Both the wrongs we have done and the wrongs done to us were nailed there with Him. It means that Jesus not only identifies with us completely in our suffering because He had an experience like ours, He also participates in our suffering because our very own experience of suffering has mysteriously been laid on Him.[11]

Can you possibly imagine what's all packed in those three little words: "who was dead"? Revelation unfolds Jesus as "the Lamb slain from the foundation of the world" (Rev. 13:8). He carried our sins and our sorrows. His substitutionary death touches the very heart of our hurts.

Our fallen world hurts and exploits people. It abuses children and oppresses the innocent. Followers of Christ face opposition and persecution. Tragedies of all kinds afflict us and the ones we love. Woundedness, it seems, is simply a fact of life. But we are not alone in our sufferings and trials. Despite our emotional, psychological, and physical injuries, Jesus has not abandoned us. Rather, He enters our painful situations to bring healing and redemption. It is important to know Christ's heart as we face suffering. In this way we may understand our experiences in light of His love for us and in light of His sharing our suffering in the cross, rather than interpreting His heart toward us on the basis of our own suffering.[12]

Jesus goes on to encourage the hurting community in Smyrna further: I am the one "who was dead, and has come to life" (Rev. 2:8, NASB). Think about those powerful words for a moment: "and has come to life." In Smyrna Christians were suffering and dying for Jesus. He wanted them to know that He had suffered and died for them first. Then He rose from the dead to guarantee that they would rise to life as well. "I am everything you need. I have everything you need. If you are faithful even to the point of death, I will give you a crown of life" (see verse 10). If you overcome, you will not be hurt by the second death (verse 11).

The crown of life is the victor's crown. It was the garland wreath placed on the head of the victorious athlete at the games or the conquering military leader. Smyrna was famous for its athletic games, so it would be a natural metaphor for John to use.

One story coming out of ancient Smyrna relates how one of the garland wreaths went posthumously to a leading citizen. In other words, although he's dead he still gets a crown of life. It fits the death-life antithesis of the passage. The Smyrnaeans bestow their honor on a corpse, while Jesus uses it to bring "life" out of death. The single major theme of this letter is that Christ will bring life out of death. Nothing they could ever suffer would fail to lead to His vindication of them and their reward. As the first and the last, the living Jesus would stand down there at the end of history—and bring life out of death.[13] In between is the incredible promise that God causes everything to work together for

the good of those who love Him and are called according to His purpose for them (Rom. 8:28). Those who follow Christ never pay a
price—not really. They invest the weight of their cross in the gain of
His everlasting kingdom.

Dennis Ngien, an international evangelist and pastor in Canada, tells
about a conversation he had with a Czech government official as he was
returning home on a plane following a preaching tour in the former
Czechoslovakia. The man had attended one of the services at which Ngien
had preached about Christ's suffering for His people. However, instead of
inspiring him to trust in God, the man left the service cursing Him, his
mind swirling around the 40 years of torment he and his family had experienced during Communist rule. He particularly remembered his parent's
death by starvation and his own wrenching years growing up in an or-
phanage. When the man arrived home after the meeting, he continued to
burn with rage. Then his eyes fell on a crucifix hanging on his apartment
wall that his mother had given him before she died. She had prayed that
someday he would come to know Christ. But seeing it fueled his anger
even more. He was so upset that he picked up a cake topped with thick
white icing and threw it at the crucifix. The cake hit the crucifix, and the
icing clung to it. Then it slowly began to drip off the face of the crucified
Jesus hanging there.

At that moment Ngien's words about Christ's suffering echoed in his
mind. As he stared intently at the figure of Jesus, he noticed that the icing
seemed to form tears in His eyes. The official was so moved by those apparent tears that he fell on his knees before the cross and surrendered his
life to Christ. "Christ is for me, not against me," he exclaimed. "I don't
understand many of the things that happened politically," the man told
Ngien as they continued to talk on the plane, "but I know that Jesus did
not forsake me. He was in pain when I was in pain. He was in tears when
I was in tears. He did not experience joy when I suffered most."[14]

Like Jenny throwing rocks or the Czech government official his cake,
we may find ourselves hurling things as we confront the intense pain of our
undeserved hurts. After all, the road to the cross is strewn with rocks and
other objects thrown by rage-filed sufferers down through the centuries.
So Christ's invitation to us still stands: "Come, walk this rugged road with
Me. Throw rocks (or a cake) if you have to. But don't turn away—keep
your eyes on Me. Consider your affliction in the light of My affliction,
your wounds in the light of Mine. Be assured that I know and understand.
You have a part. I have a part. Be faithful unto death [your part] and I will

give you the crown of life [My part]. He who overcomes [your part] will not be hurt by the second death [My part]" (see verses 10, 11).

Our compassionate Jesus meets us in every corner of our lives. Because He knows pain firsthand, we can pray with confidence that He will be moved by our cries. Jesus suffers with us because He wills to love us. A love that does not agonize with the suffering of the beloved is not love at all.

How He answers our prayers is a matter of His wisdom and sovereignty. And we may submit to whatever is His decision with the assurance that He hugs us close to Him as His beloved. We can assure our hearts that He was in agony for us on the cross as He carried our sins and our sorrows. He feels for me and is with me still. Jesus cares. And that, surely, is the best news ever.

That's why I love Jesus! I love Him because He knows my sorrows and trials. He not only knows what I am going through right now—He also knows what I will go through tomorrow. And not only does He know and care; He has everything I need to be at peace and remain faithful. He invests my suffering in a hope-filled future.

---

[1] Osborne, *Revelation*, pp. 129, 130.

[2] John R. W. Stott, *What Christ Thinks of the Church: Insights From Revelation 2-3* (Grand Rapids: William B. Eerdmans, 1958), p. 39.

[3] *Documents Illustrative of the History of the Church: Vol. I to A.D. 313*, ed. B. J. Kidd (New York: Macmillan Co., 1938), pp. 64-72.

[4] Osborne, p. 136.

[5] *Ibid.*

[6] Doukhan, *Secrets of Revelation*, p. 194.

[7] We likely find here an allusion to Jeremiah 51:49 that blames Babylon not only for the slaughter of Israelites but also for that of other peoples as well: "Babylon must fall for the slain of Israel, as for Babylon have fallen the slain of all the earth" (see David E. Aune, *Revelation 17-22*, Word Biblical Commentary, vol. 52c [Nashville: Thomas Nelson, 1998], p. 1011; Osborne, p. 659).

[8] Osborne, p. 136.

[9] Frank Lake, *Clinical Theology* (London: Darton, Longman and Todd, 1966), p. 116.

[10] Stephen Seamands, *Wounds That Heal: Bringing Our Hurts to the Cross* (Downers Grove, Ill.: InterVarsity Press, 2003), p. 17.

[11] *Ibid.*, p. 18.

[12] Keener, *Revelation*, p. 120.

[13] Osborne, p. 135.

[14] Dennis Ngien, "The God Who Suffers," *Christianity Today*, Feb. 3, 1997, p. 42.

CHAPTER 7

I LOVE JESUS BECAUSE . . .

HE HELPS ME WIN

Nike Every Day—"Just Do It!"
Revelation 3:21

The Nike Company swung into action even before most Chinese knew they had a new hero. The moment hurdler Liu Xiang became the country's first Olympic medalist in a short-distance speed event—he claimed the gold in a new Olympic record in the 110-meter hurdles at the Greece Summer Olympics on August 28, 2004—Nike launched a television advertisement in China showing Liu destroying the field and superimposed a series of questions designed to set nationalistic teeth on edge: "Asians lack muscle? Asians lack the will to win?" Then came the kicker. As Liu raised his arms above the trademark Swoosh on his shoulder the words shot across the screen: "Stereotypes are made to be broken." It was an instant marketing success.

"Nike understands why Chinese are proud," one weekend player said at a Swoosh-bedecked basketball court near Beijing's Tiananmen Square. Such clever marketing tactics have helped make Nike the icon for the new China. According to a survey, Chinese consider Nike the Middle Kingdom's "coolest brand"—a symbol defining success for the nation's new middle class. The company was smart because it didn't enter China just selling usefulness. Rather, it marketed status and a creative new lifestyle. The brand offered a sense of personal identity, value, and being. One of Beijing's leading DJs credited the company with "making me the person I am."[1]

REVELATION'S GREAT LOVE STORY

We like to share the symbols of victory or vicariously identify with them. Consider the people who rushed to purchase Red Sox paraphernalia after their historic comeback. The team had been behind 3-0 in the playoffs against the New York Yankees, but then thoroughly stomped the Cardinals 4-0 in the 2004 World Series. Their victory was sweet after being losers year after year since 1918.

Victory is a recurring theme in the Apocalypse and one of the book's key motifs (Rev. 2:7, 11, 17, 26; 3:5, 12, 21; 5:5; 12:11; 15:2; 17:14; 21:7).[2] It is so central that Jesus links it to His own experience and privilege: "He who overcomes, I will grant to him to sit down with Me on My throne, *as I also overcame and sat down* with My Father on His throne" (Rev. 3:21, NASB). The Greek word for "overcome" is *nikáo,* which means "to be a victor, to be victorious, to overcome, to conquer." Nike is the noun form. In Greek mythology the goddess Nike (originally pronounced "nee kay") was the personification of victory. Images of the deity were popular in Greek culture. Exquisite reliefs of the goddess graced the temple of Athena Nike on the Athenian Acropolis. Roman mythology called her Victoria. Her powers extended to many areas of ancient Greek life, including athletics. Perhaps that is why the legendary shoe and sports paraphernalia manufacturer borrowed the name of the goddess for its corporate identity and marketing strategy.

The form of the verb Jesus uses when He says "he who overcomes" (a present active participle) implies continuous overcoming or continuous victory. It is not *overcame*—as if it happened in the past or is something accomplished—but *overcome* as a pattern of life. It points to people's self-identity, their *being.* They are *overcomers!* The book of Revelation primarily employs the image of conquering as a militaristic one closely connected to the language of battle (Rev. 11:7; 12:7, 8, 17; 13:7; 16:14; 17:14; 19:11, 19).[3] Overcoming in the Apocalypse is no mere game.

Revelation's call to conquer is fundamental to its structure and theme, and the book applies the concept to both Jesus (Rev. 3:21; 5:5; 17:14) and His people (Rev. 2:7, 11, 17, 26; 3:5, 12, 21; 12:11; 15:2; 21:7). Within the Apocalypse the followers of Christ repeat (though with vast qualitative difference) His experience in the world and reflect His character. Christ's final words to the lukewarm church of Laodicea asserts the "overcomer's" moral affinity with the person, character, and work of Jesus. It is the first time that the Apocalypse compares the saints' overcoming with that of Christ's.[4] Such overcoming and the rights that accompany it represent an explicit linking of Christology and ethics in the Apocalypse.[5] Ultimately, overcoming demands the reader's active participation in the divine war against evil. Everything said in the seven messages to the churches has this aim in mind.[6]

The Winner's Circle

Winners have privileges! They get to pick up the spoils of battle (or the rewards of the game or contest) and celebrate afterward. Or they get to run with the trophy or wear the prized ring, wreath, or medal. Theirs are the rewards and accolades and distinction. Winning is fun and satisfying.

The book of Revelation enumerates a long list of the winners' privileges. Jesus promises "the one who overcomes" (as a present ongoing experience) the future reward of sharing His throne—just as He overcame and sat with the Father on His throne (Rev. 3:21). Sitting on a throne was a great privilege in John's day. But it is not your average throne that Jesus has in mind— not even Rome's coveted throne on which Caesar sat. It is the throne of the living God (Rev. 4). The throne from which He sovereignly reigns over all—both heaven and earth. The symbolism of throne is a major emphasis in Revelation which contrasts the "throne of God" with the "throne of Satan" (Rev. 12:5 contra Rev. 13:2; cf. Rev. 2:13; 16:10) and probably with Caesar's throne as well.[7] Thrones always symbolize the power and rule and judgment of the sovereigns who sit on them. Scripture could give no better symbol of the privilege of victory.

Winner privileges appear throughout the letters to the seven churches:

Ephesus: "To him who overcomes, I will grant to eat of the tree of life which is in the Paradise of God" (Rev. 2:7, NASB).

Smyrna: "He who overcomes will not be hurt by the second death" (verse 11, NASB).

Pergamum: "To him who overcomes, to him I will give *some* of the hidden manna, and I will give him a white stone, and a new name written on the stone which no one knows but he who receives it" (verse 17, NASB).

Thyatira: "He who overcomes, and he who keeps My deeds until the end, to him I will give authority over the nations; and he shall rule them with a rod of iron, as the vessels of the potter are broken to pieces, as I also have received *authority* from My Father; and I will give him the morning star" (verses 26-28, NASB).

Sardis: "He who overcomes will thus be clothed in white garments; and I will not erase his name from the book of life, and I will confess his name before My Father and before His angels" (Rev. 3:5, NASB).

Philadelphia: "He who overcomes, I will make him a pillar in the temple of My God, and he will not go out from it anymore; and I will write on him the name of My God, and the name of the city of My God, the new Jerusalem, which comes down out of heaven from My God, and My new name" (verse 12, NASB).

Laodicea: "He who overcomes, I will grant to him to sit down with Me on My throne, as I also overcame and sat down with My Father on His throne" (verse 21, NASB).

The rewards for the victorious are striking: access to the tree of life in a restored Eden (Ephesus); security against the second death (Smyrna); intimacy with Christ and admission to heaven (Pergamum); participation in Christ's victory over all hostile entities as well as having Christ Himself who will end the long night of sin's rule in the universe (Thyatira); wearing white robes with Christ in triumphant victory procession at the eschaton; having one's name remain on the Lamb's list, and having Christ brag on you before the Father and His angels (Sardis); stability and security in the very presence of God, who is eternally with His people (Philadelphia); and identity with Christ as a fellow overcomer, together with the privilege of reigning with Him forever (Laodicea).

Near Revelation's close we find one more promise: "He who overcomes will inherit these things, and I will be his God and he will be My son" (Rev. 21:7, NASB). Here we come face to face with God's gracious covenant blessing. He will faithfully fulfill all His promises. Everything He has promised in terms of an earth made new—one with no death, sorrow, suffering, pain, or crying—will be finally and forever realized (verse 4). God makes all things new (verse 5). The overcomer not only inherits it all, but experiences the Lord's personal presence forever (cf. Rev. 21:3; 22:4).

Revelation's winner's circle has awesome privileges.

Getting It Right

But what does it mean to overcome? And what are we supposed to overcome? More important, how do we overcome?

Jesus wants us to overcome in those areas of life that really matter. He longs for us to be successful in those everyday struggles that define who we really are: how we feel, our habits, our attitudes, our choices, our values and behavior—in other words, our character. Christ seeks for us to be victorious in those spiritual and moral realities that determine eternity. Whenever we face trials, opposition, temptations, fear, or spiritual/moral compromise, He wants us to be an overcomer.

Revelation gives us insight into some of those areas of life that really matter, as well as what it means to overcome. First, overcoming has moral implications. We catch a glimpse of this near the close of the book when God declares that "he who overcomes will inherit these things, and I will be his God and he will be My son. But for the cowardly and unbelieving and abominable and murderers and immoral persons and sorcerers and idolaters and all liars, their part *will be* in the lake that burns with fire and brimstone, which is the second death" (Rev. 22:7, 8, NASB). Similar imagery appears when John is told, "Blessed are those who wash their robes, so that they may have the right to the tree of life, and may enter by the gates into the city. Outside are the dogs and the sorcerers and the immoral persons and the murderers and the idolaters, and everyone who loves and practices lying" (Rev. 22:14, 15, NASB).

Such solemn warnings about those who will find themselves barred from the winner's circle (the earth made new and the Holy City) seek to encourage readers to examine their own lives accordingly (cf. Rev. 9:20, 21; 21:27). Those on the roster of outcasts and outsiders have "been overcome" by their fears or unbelief or idolatry; their sexual passions; their hatred; their fascination with magic and the occult; or their hoodwinking of others (lying and loving to lie). Overcoming implies such things as sexual integrity, courage, faith and faithfulness, love, a forgiving spirit, loyalty to and worship of God alone, and truthfulness, to name just a few.

Christ's words to the seven churches show how overcoming covers a wide range of moral and spiritual issues (Rev. 2:7, 11, 17, 26; 3:5, 12, 21). The letters allude to several threats to authentic worship of God (Rev. 1:9–3:21).[8] We find references to the "synagogue of Satan" (Rev. 2:9; 3:9); "Satan's throne" (Rev. 2:13, NASB); the eating of food offered to idols (verse 14); and a false prophet, Jezebel (verse 20). Each allusion suggests some kind of practical (thus detectable) compromise to Christian worship, a pollution of the purity of the church, or a threat from external religious or secular forces. Here overcoming includes such things as sexual morality (verse 22; cf. verse 21); practical first-love expressions (verse 5); and actions that both determine reputation as an authentic worshipping community (Rev. 3:1) and that completely carries out God's will in both quantity and quality (verse 2).[9] It also encompasses the practical moral realities of keeping Christ's Word (verse 8; cf. verse 10), of not denying His name (verse 8), and of maintaining spiritual passion (verse 15). Overcoming refers to the whole walk of the believer, as defined by the contents of the churches' "deeds" (*erga*) referred to in the letters (Rev. 2:2, 3, 5, 6, 19, 22, 23, 26;

3:1, 2, 8, 15).[10] Such "deeds" have to do with what the churches are *doing* or *not doing* right.[11]

When the matter of worship comes to a head with the demand to worship the beast in chapters 12-14, moral action and ethical practice are at the very heart of the conflict—keeping the commandments of God (Rev. 12:17; 14:12). The recurring theme of "keeping" (*tēreō*) appears nine times in the Apocalypse and comprises one of the major ethical themes of the book (Rev. 1:3; 2:26; 3:8, 10; 12:17; 14:12; 16:15; 22:7, 9).[12] The word includes both the basic ethical principle of perseverance (i.e., maintain, hold on to, keep on, continue) and obedience (i.e., heed, obey, observe, comply with, follow, do). The book defines "keeping" in relation to God's instructions, i.e., "the words of this prophecy" (Rev. 1:3; 22:7; cf. Rev. 22:18, 19), "My deeds" (Rev. 2:26, NASB), "the commandments of God" (Rev. 12:17; 14:12), "the words of this book" (Rev. 22:9, NASB; cf. 22:18, 19), as well as the "faith of Jesus" (Rev. 14:12). Overcoming thus encompasses very concrete and observable dimensions. It is has the force of holding fast a confession (of faith and obedience) when facing false doctrine, when experiencing incredible pressure, and when meeting a martyr's death.

Second, overcoming in Revelation is the ability to both discern and hold on to God-given truth in the face of masterful delusion and unprecedented coercion. "I saw something like a sea of glass mixed with fire, and those who had been victorious [overcome] over the beast and his image and the number of his name, standing on the sea of glass, holding harps of God," writes John (Rev. 15:2, NASB). In the last half of the book Revelation unfolds a massive and relentless spiritual and moral force that nearly overwhelms reality and truth with its deceptions (Rev. 13:14; 18:23; 19:20). Those who dwell on the earth encounter powerful spiritual (and doctrinal), sociopolitical, cultural, even demonic forces that fundamentally alter their sense of what is, in fact, spiritually or morally right and wrong. For example, we find the devil, "who deceives the whole world" (Rev. 12:9; see also Rev. 20:3, 8, 10). The second beast of chapter 13—the one from the earth—deludes the inhabitants of the earth with his propaganda about the first beast and the supernatural signs that he is able to perform (Rev. 13:14; 19:20). And we encounter the great prostitute's [Babylon] gold cup filled with intoxicating wine of false teachings. She has made people drunk by deceiving the world with her sorceries (Rev. 17:1-5; 18:23). The prostitute imagery highlights Babylon's deceptive nature as an object of desire that in reality kills (Prov. 2:16-19; 6:24-32; 7:9-23).

During the reign of the devil, the beast, and the false prophet (Revelation's trinity of evil), the earth is an arena of deceit and illusion (Rev. 16:13, 14; cf. Rev. 13:13, 14; 19:20; 12:9; 20:3, 8, 10). The evil trinity causes people to become spiritually disoriented. Fallen humanity thinks that it is doing right when in fact it is doing wrong. Human beings assume that they know truth when in reality lies now guide their existence. They have only a shattered visage of God, the truth about Him, or how He would have human beings live.

Naturally, one of Revelation's dominant concerns is with truth and deception, transforming the world into a kind of courtroom to decide the issue of who is the true God and what is truth.[13] Revelation focuses both on the truth about God and the truth of God.[14] In the process the Apocalypse teaches us that ideas have consequences, that wrong ideas are dangerous, and that truth matters. Being truthful and being true are vital. Revelation promises hope in the unveiling of truth in Jesus Christ (Rev. 1:1).

But the conflict between truth and error involves more than delusion. Error employs coercion, intimidation, persecution, and the threat of death (Rev. 2:9, 10; 11:3-13; 13:7, 15; 17:6; 18:24). While the character of the conflict will be verbal and ideological—a battle for the mind and moral vision by means of bewitching persuasion—it will include physical force.[15] Overcoming the beast and his image and the number of his name (Rev. 15:2) will take place in the face of these confusing and terrorizing realities. It means first being able to discern the truth and then holding onto it no matter the cost—even that of death itself (Rev. 12:11).

Third, overcoming means choosing right values and associations. Revelation 18 provides an incredible picture of fallen human civilization in all of its varied aspects. It is religious but independent of God, and it blossoms for one last time as a splendid city called Babylon. Babylon is a great wicked metropolis, the capital of antichrist, the persecutor of God's people. The book of Revelation characterizes it as an extravagant, drunken prostitute, riding a monstrous beast (Rev. 17:1-6, 18). The city of Babylon depicts the complete control of the political, religious, commercial, and cultural apparatus of society by the satanic power structure (Rev. 13; 17; 18). This has been true at significant moments in history, both in John's time and during the Christian age, and it will especially be the case in the time leading up to the end.

We're accustomed to reading Revelation 18 exclusively from the standpoint of the religious/moral fall of professing Christianity within

101

history until the end of time. We need to notice, though, how the same chapter announces the single biggest financial meltdown that the world will ever experience: "for in one hour such great wealth has been laid waste!" (Rev. 18:17, NASB). When this end-time economic crash happens, the earth's merchants will mourn because no one will buy their cargo anymore (verse 11). The chapter's emphasis upon luxury goods reveals the self-indulgent value system of the rebellious order and the greedy manipulation of the merchants who use it for their own gain (verses 12, 13). The merchants were the world's great men and women who had every opportunity to use their influence for good instead of for self and evil (verses 23, 24). Human beings themselves, however, have become a commodity in a value system that thinks only of material gain and well-being (verses 13, 24).

/ Babylon then, in part at least, is a world of buying and selling (as well as a religious/moral reality). According to this chapter, buying and selling is the ultimate value for those who dwell on the earth (cf. Rev. 13:17). Such buying and selling becomes of more value than worshipping the God of heaven by obeying His commandments (Rev. 12:17; 14:12).

It is important to note how Revelation reveals that overcoming does not mean conquering Babylon. Rather, it involves withdrawing from all that she stands for and does in the world: "I heard another voice from heaven, saying, 'Come out of her, my people, so that you will not participate in her sins and receive of her plagues'" (Rev. 18:4, NASB). Overcoming involves not only holding a different set of values (justice, equity, stewardship, generosity, simplicity, spirituality, truthfulness, true biblical teaching and spiritual life, etc.), but consciously and publicly disassociating one's self from a corrupt culture and religious institutions that link sensuality, immorality, consumerism, religious compromise, the demonic, and mood-altering substances (verses 2, 3, 7, 9, 14).[16] Thus, overcoming includes such things as values, association, and moral choice in which the ultimate value is identifying with God and His principles as well as honoring His commandments (Rev. 14:12; cf. Rev. 18:4). The Lord does not want His people to participate in Babylon's sins. Rather, He calls for them to be fundamentally different in character and life.

Fourth, we are to overcome Satan himself. The book of Revelation everywhere assumes and asserts that Satan actively wars against God's people (Rev. 2:9, 10, 13, 24; 3:9; 12:4, 9, 13, 15-17; 20:10). It also states that believers in Jesus Christ actually defeat both Satan and his accusations: "And they overcame him because of the blood of the Lamb and because of the word of their testimony, and they did not love their life even when faced with death" (Rev. 12:11, NASB; cf. verse 10). Such a victory is almost unimaginable were it not for the blood of the Lamb, and yet faithful testimony in the midst of withering opposition and the willingness to give up one's life for Christ spells yet another defeat for the archenemy.

Finally, we are to overcome as Jesus did: "[To the one] who overcomes, I will grant . . . to sit down with Me on My throne, *as I also overcame* and sat down with my Father on His throne" (Rev. 3:21, NASB). We should not pass over the words "as I also overcame" too quickly. Here is the first time that the Apocalypse compares the saints' overcoming to Christ's overcoming.[17] This overcoming and the rights that accompany it represent an explicit linking of Christology (the study of Christ) and ethics (moral philosophy) in the Apocalypse.[18] There is more here than just overcoming. It is overcoming *in the same way* that Jesus did. The overcoming itself is not as important as the way in which individuals overcome and what they overcome.

As one of Revelation's important transitional passages, these words of comparison (Rev. 3:21) function as the introductory passage for the next eight chapters (4-11), and chapters 4-7 in particular.[19] Chapter 5 especially develops the theme of "overcoming" in the seven churches (2:1-3:21), where it has its natural transition at Revelation 3:21.[20] There in chapter 5 we find John's vision of the slaughtered Lamb who overcomes in an astounding and unexpected way. John hears that "the Lion of the tribe of Judah, the Root of David" had conquered (Rev. 5:5, NKJV). But when he turns to look, he sees a lamb standing as if slain (verse 6). He expects a powerful lion who tears his prey (Ps. 17:12), but discovers a torn lamb instead. There is violence, but it is endured violence, not inflicted violence. Yet the Lamb has conquered. It has displayed moral power rather than coercive physical power. The Lamb's sacrificial death (Rev. 5:6) has redeemed people from all nations (verses 9, 10). Jesus the Messiah has won an incredible victory, but He has done so by sacrifice, not by coercive force or military violence. Jesus conquered through suffering and weakness rather than by either human or divine might. This scene lies at the theological (and thus ethical) heart of the Apocalypse.[21]

His own self-sacrificing victory thus turns out to be *a way of being in the world*—a model for believers, i.e., "as I also overcame."[22] Within the Apocalypse the followers of Christ repeat (though with vast qualitative difference) Christ's experience in the world and reflect His character (Rev. 6:9, 10; 11:3-13; 12; etc.). Their self-sacrifice, innocent sufferings, steadfast endurance, martyrdom, and faithful witness in behalf of Christ and for a lost world have saving influence on the nations. We will touch on this more later, but for now we must see that at bottom overcoming is to be like Jesus in the world. It means being willing to be like the little seed that dies in order that a harvest can be reaped (John 12:24-33).

Self-sacrifice is powerful, moving people and melting hearts. Suffering has moral power for what is right (Rev. 2:10; 6:9-11; 12:10, 11; 11:3-13). The simple voicing of one's own testimony about Jesus (Rev. 12:11) can dramatically affect things. Denying self for the sake of Jesus and for the sake of others is what overcoming is all about. Death to self is both the greatest battle and the most profound victory.

When we put all these things together, we get a distinct sense that the Apocalypse regards overcoming as a victory involving one's entire life.[23]

All of us like to win. Most of all we like to triumph where it really matters: in those spiritual and moral realities that determine eternity—truthfulness, faithfulness, love, purity, honesty, faith, etc. We long for victory in that subtle battle for the mind waged by bewitching ideas, allowing nothing to coerce us either psychologically or physically. Withstanding the beast and his image and all that we understand that to mean, we want both to discern truth and to hold on to it with our very life. Our dream is to triumph over Satan, remaining faithful to Christ in both word and life, even if it means death. And we would win that one, too—being faithful unto death (Rev. 2:10; 12:11). Most of all, we want to be selfless and self-sacrificing for others like Jesus. This is true victory!

Sometimes, though, we feel so weak and vulnerable, not knowing which way to turn or how much longer we can take it. Holding on is hard and spiritually exhausting. Overcoming the way that Revelation describes is not easy. Winning demands something that we often don't have in ourselves. It's so easy to become defeated by life or by one's own self. When life overwhelms us, it hurts. While it's one thing to lose a game, it's quite another to lose at life—your marriage, your job, some substance or habit, fear or weakness, whatever. When we experience defeat again and again in those areas that really matter, we become discouraged and wonder about ourselves. Before long we conclude that religion doesn't work for us. During such moments all the rewards held out for the winner's circle seem so incredibly distant. Overcoming can be hard! Just hearing how important overcoming is in the Apocalypse can easily create a feeling that there's a lot more that we need to be and do than we can ever possibly accomplish.

The Victory of the Lamb

A group of seminary students played basketball after classes at a nearby high school playground. Nearly every day an elderly, white-haired janitor would come out and watch them. After a while he'd sit down on the steps of the building, get out an old, tattered Bible, and read it. The students couldn't help noticing him. One day one of the seminarians walked over to the old janitor and asked, "What are you reading?"

"The Bible," he replied.

"I know that. What book?"

"The book of Revelation."

"Revelation! Do you understand it?"

"Sure, I understand it," the janitor said confidently.

The aspiring young minister was a bit taken aback that this simple man claimed to understand the most complex book in the Bible. So he challenged him. "All right, then, what does it mean?"

"It means," the man answered with a grin, "we win!"

That's exactly what Revelation says. We win in the end: over our fears, whatever they are; over our enemies, whoever they are. The message of Revelation is that simple. But the reason we win is that Jesus does: "And the Lamb shall overcome them: for he is Lord of lords, and King of kings: and they that are with him *are* called, and chosen, and faithful" (Rev. 17:14). That's why I love Jesus. He helps me win!

The book of Revelation announces the worldwide scope of Christ's complete victory. He is the celebrated Lamb who has overcome and as "King of kings and Lord of lords" finally overcomes (Rev. 3:21; 5:5; 17:14). Ultimate victory is with Jesus and Him alone. The book uses the language of conquering for all the three stages of Christ's work. He conquered in His death and resurrection (Rev. 3:21; 5:5), He conquers through His followers in the time before the end (Rev. 12:11; 15:2), and He will conquer when He appears the second time (Rev. 1:7; 17:14; 19:17-21).[24]

Almost dead center of the book a loud voice in heaven announces (with triumphant song) victory over Satan's rule, the inauguration of God's reign in the world, and Christ's kingly authority:[25] "Then I heard a loud voice in heaven, saying, 'Now the salvation, and the power, and the kingdom of our God and the authority of His Christ have come, for the accuser of our brethren has been thrown down, he who accuses them before our God day and night. And they overcame him because of the blood of the Lamb and because of the word of their testimony, and they did not love their life even when faced with death. For this reason, rejoice, O heavens and you who dwell in them. Woe to the earth and the sea, because the devil has come down to you, having great wrath, knowing that he has *only* a short time" (Rev. 12:10-12). A hymn celebrating God's mighty actions on behalf of human beings, it tells us how effectively Jesus wins and how we share in His victory.

The first stanza of this victory song begins with the temporal adverb "now." The word refers to the longed-for time when: (1) salvation and power and the kingdom of God replaces Satan's usurping rule and abuse of power; (2) Christ's moral authority is forever established; and (3) the incessant accuser Satan finally gets expelled from heavenly places (Rev. 12:10; cf. John 12:31-33; Luke 10:17, 19, 20). In other words: "It has happened at last" (NLT). Jesus wins. The hymn does not just anticipate victory, but announces it as a present reality.

We know from the rest of the New Testament that Christ decisively vanquished the devil at the cross, and that the resurrection vindicated His victory.[26] Jesus announced just before His crucifixion: " 'Now judgment is upon this world; now the ruler of this world will be cast out. And I, if I am lifted up from the earth, will draw all men to Myself.' But He was saying this to indicate the kind of death by which He was to die" (John 12:31-33). The same thing is what is in mind, too, in Revelation 5 in which the slain Lamb has overcome and is worthy to take the sealed scroll and open it (Rev. 5:5-12).

The hymn's imagery, then, refers to when Jesus suffered and died on a cross outside of Jerusalem and subsequently rose from the dead.[27] It encompasses His enthronement as both Lord and Christ following His ascension to heaven, which took place at Pentecost (Acts 2:32-36) and is portrayed in Revelation 4; 5.[28] Explaining the significance of Christ's substitutionary death and resurrection, the hymn celebrates the fact that the kingdom has begun immediately.[29] The sacrifice of Christ's life nullifies the accusations of Satan (Rev. 1:5; 5:6-9; cf. Rom. 8:1, 33, 34, 38). God is able to forgive, and His kingdom is preserved.[30]

The second stanza declares how the decisive victory of Christ on the cross becomes the basis for the victory that human beings win over Satan throughout history: "And they overcame him because of the blood of the Lamb and because of the word of their testimony, and they did not love their life even when faced with death" (Rev. 12:11, NASB). Instead of defeating the followers of Christ by accusing them, Satan suffers his own defeat. Their victory over him comes by virtue of what Christ has accomplished on the cross. Christ's blood produces the victory. The real basis for all spiritual and moral victory is always the cross, rather than a person's own strength.[31] Thus Revelation's true theme is not military battles or political events, but rather the final conquest of sin and Satan by the slain Lamb.[32] In the Lamb's blood we find sure victory. Christ's death in the Apocalypse is an event of the past as well as a present reality that every believer in Him can experience.

The victory over Satan is also a result of the faithful witness of God's people to Christ and the gospel. Their confession is both personal and other-oriented. It is personal in that the reason for their victory is their conscious choice to identify with the death of Jesus on their behalf.[33] They each have a distinct, intelligent knowledge of what their salvation cost. That is why they keep dipping their robes in the blood of the Lamb (Rev. 7:14; 22:12). And it is why they follow the Lamb in sacrificial life—surrendered in a rhythm of obedience to the Father (Rev. 12:17; 14:1-5, 12). As a result they receive both forgiveness and the moral power to be different from the world. Thus they overcome existentially.[34] People are released from their bondage to the power and penalty of sin by identifying through faith with Jesus's sacrificial death (Rev. 1:5, 6; 5:9, 10).[35] Despite intense resistance they have continued to believe in, and continued testifying to, the Lamb's substitutionary death on *their* behalf.

Their confession is other-oriented in that it is both a lifestyle of faithfulness to Christ and a verbal gospel witness during extremely difficult times (Rev. 12:17; 14:12). It spells out yet another defeat for Satan in the spiritual moral war. He not only fails to stop their faithfulness and witness, but also is unable to block the moral spiritual impact such witness has upon others. Their steadfast lifestyle becomes a means of winning people from lies and illusion to truth and to Christ (Rev. 14:6-12; 7:9, 10; 18:1-5). As they persevere in facing opposition, they are victorious. In fact, their willingness to give up their lives for Christ is the greatest victory of all.[36]

The third part of this hymn (Rev. 12:12) relates the results for heaven and earth. It leads to both rejoicing and warning. The rejoicing results from the complete and final expulsion of the dragon from the heavenly realm. However, lest Revelation's hearers become too elated, the hymn brings them back to the reality of their situation. The war still rages. Satan is still here. Verse 12 pronounces a woe because the devil will now concentrate his efforts on causing chaos among earth's inhabitants. His "great wrath" over losing his position in heaven now fuels his wrath. But his anger is sparked above all by his knowledge that he "has only a short time." The expression "a short time" indicates an expectation of the imminent consummation of the kingdom of God and Satan's final defeat. The song ends on this note of encouragement: the dragon knows that his time is short.[37] Indicating quality, not quantity, the reference to time reminds us that evil is not infinite or eternal.[38] Evil and the demonic will ultimately face defeat not only in heaven but also on earth.

The theme of the futility of Satan is central to Revelation's literary center.[39] The book pictures him as already defeated in heaven (Rev. 12:7-12), at the birth of Christ (verses 1-6), and at the cross (verses 11, 12; cf. Rev. 5:6). His rage stems not so much from his hatred of God as from his defeat by Christ. Everything Satan does is merely a parody of what God has already done or will do.[40] Believers participate in this great victory over Satan even through their suffering. Every time Satan conquers them through persecution (Rev. 13:7) they conquer him by not loving their lives "so much as to shrink from death" (Rev. 12:11, NIV). We find no portrayal of the dragon as an ultimate powerful being.[41] His victories are both earthly and temporal, while his defeats are final and eternal.

Occurring at almost the literary center of the Apocalypse, this awe-inspiring hymn comprises Revelation's theological center and represents in symbolic fashion the fulcrum point of salvation history:[42] Jesus wins, and then He helps us to win.

Is This You?

Part of Nike's marketing strategy has been unabashedly to make American culture its selling point with ads that challenge China's traditional, group-oriented ethos. The company released internet teaser clips showing a faceless but Asian-looking high school basketball player shaking-and-baking his way through a formidable defense. Timed to coincide with Nike tournaments around the country, it concluded with the question "Is this you?"[43]

Nike wanted every Chinese young person to envision their own face on that faceless, conquering player. "Is this you?" it asked. "It can be!" the teaser implied.

Revelation reports how "they overcame him [Satan] because of the blood of the Lamb and because of the word of their testimony, and they did not love their life even when faced with death" (Rev. 12:11, NASB). The victorious *they* that the book describes are both faceless and nameless. John does not tell us who *they* are. Only that *they* overcome. Undoubtedly *they* are the faithful of every age since the cross, especially those who have experienced tribulation for their belief in and commitment to Jesus Christ.

Like the Nike Company, John wants us to imagine our own face on those faceless, conquering *theys*. "Is this you?" Revelation asks every reader. Why not? It can be. But how? "Just do it!" as Nike asserts? As if you've got it in you and just need to apply yourself? Do we "just do it!"? No, because according to Revelation, "He's done it!" Our victory over Satan (and every other facet of Revelation's overcoming as outlined above) comes by virtue of what Jesus has accomplished on the cross. The blood of Christ produces the victory. The real basis for all spiritual and moral victory in our lives has always been and always will be the cross rather than any strength of our own.

So then, how do we overcome existentially?[44] First, we do that when we personally identify with the substitutionary atonement of Jesus Christ in our behalf (Rev. 12:11). Second, we overcome when we openly bear witness to the cross and give testimony of our own faith in Christ and how His substitutionary death has forever changed our lives (verse 11). Third, we overcome when we will cling to the cross no matter what comes even if it means physical death (verse 11). And finally, we overcome by continually dipping our robes in the white-bleaching blood of the Lamb (Rev. 7:14; 22:14). That is *how* we receive both forgiveness and moral power to be different from the world. /

Revelation points to the need for character and life to be immersed in the substitutionary work of Jesus. People find themselves released from their bondage to the power and penalty of sin only by identifying through faith with Jesus' sacrificial death (Rev. 1:5, 6; 5:9; 12:11).[45] The redeemed will go through the great tribulation by identifying by faith with Jesus' sacrificial death (Rev. 7:14). Their reaction to temptations to compromise and to the threat of oppression and tribulation has been to continue to trust in the Lamb, who both bought them by His blood and released them from their sins with it (Rev. 1:5; 5:9). Despite intense pressure they have continued to believe in and testify to the Lamb's substitutionary death on their behalf. The reason for their victory over the world is the death of Jesus and their conscious choice to identify with it.[46]

What will keep us faithful to Jesus now or anytime in the future? It's the cross. It alone will enable us to grasp the real issues behind the trinity of evil's juggernaut. Only the cross will lead us toward moral excellence or a self-sacrificing life or to associate with Jesus and the values of His kingdom. Those who will receive the seal of God will be those who realize that it is only through the shed blood of Jesus that they will ever make it though the final crisis (Rev. 7:1-15). We won't honor the Sabbath (or any other commandment) just because it's right or because God asked us to obey it. Rather, we will follow the Lamb wherever He leads and no matter what He asks us to be, because we know that we are a lost sinner for whom Jesus Christ has died. We will surrender our personal lifestyle choices only because we have a deep sense of what it means to be redeemed by the blood of the Lamb. Behind every act of obedience to God or moment of faithfulness stands a sense of the cross and a deep personal understanding of what it means to be saved by the blood of Jesus Christ.

Speaking of the redeemed, Ellen White writes that "by their own painful experience they learned the evil of sin, its power, its guilt, its woe; and they look upon it with abhorrence. A sense of the infinite sacrifice made for its cure humbles them in their own sight and fills their hearts with gratitude and praise which those who have never fallen cannot appreciate. They love much because they have been forgiven much."[47]

Is this you? It can be. Victory is a promise held out to each of the seven churches, even to the weak ones, such as Sardis and Laodicea. Revelation implies that the Christian life is not only a warfare from which there is no discharge, but also a conflict in which even the feeblest can prove victorious.[48] How gracious Jesus is. And how wonderful the promise.

Whenever I recite Revelation (usually on a walk to keep it fresh in my mind), I always anticipate certain verses and enjoy verbalizing them with a fully engaged heart. I want to utter the images they express as powerful truths that I really believe, or want to confess again, or desire to experience for myself. One of these special passages appears in Revelation 17. There John writes of the last-day 10 kings who turn over their influence and power fully to the dreaded beast and subsequently join with the beast in waging war against the Lamb (Rev. 17:12-14; cf. Rev. 19:19). But John says that "the Lamb will overcome them, because He is Lord of lords and King of kings" (Rev. 7:14, NASB). I like that promise and enjoy savoring it in my thoughts. The Lamb will overcome them—and every other challenging force I read about in the Apocalypse.

But it doesn't end there. What comes next is just as exciting: "and those who are with Him *are the* called and chosen and faithful" (verse 14, NASB). John tells us who will share in the Lamb's victory—"those who are *with* Him." The little preposition "with" seems like such an unimportant word. It's easy to miss what "with" says about overcoming. When Jesus overcomes, those who are *with* Him share His victory. They overcome *with* Him. We should not understand the four-letter preposition in terms of spacial proximity or physical accompaniment, but relationally in terms of faith and faithfulness, identity and connection. Their designation as "faithful" indicates the fulfillment of the human response by those who share Christ's victory.[49] Being an overcomer involves a day-by-day walk with Jesus and dependence on His strength. It means placing living for Him above all earthly things. We don't *use* Jesus to give us an edge or to guarantee victory. He's not like a performance-enhancing drug or piece of equipment. Rather, He is a person who has overcome and shares His incredible victory with those who have chosen Him as Lord and Savior.

When I try to figure out how my *being with* Jesus helps me overcome in my ordinary life, I think of one of those enormous rocks I have seen during hikes in the mountains. Rather, two rocks that used to be one, but is now split in two. And it is clear what caused the split.

Long ago water seeped into a crevice, froze, and created a deeper opening. Then a seed blew into the deepened crack and germinated. From that tiny seed a tree began to grow, sending its strong roots deeper and deeper into that crack and all along its surface until its inexorable growth simply pushed the rock apart. Now there are two rocks and a tree right in the middle. That's power—quiet, indefatigable, and the kind of energy you sense even if you can't see it.

When I choose to be with Him—daily claiming His blood, owning His values, openly confessing Him before others, and ever keeping my eyes on Him—He breaks up things and starts something new. It's power that I can't see or explain, but simply experience through His grace—because I am *with* Him. Things that are impossible with me are possible with Jesus (Luke 18:27). "This is the victory that has overcome the world—our faith" (1 John 5:4, NASB). "You . . . have overcome them; because greater is He who is in you than he who is in the world" (1 John 4:4, NASB).

Is this you? Are you an overcomer?

Jesus wins! And because He does, I can too. When I'm defeated by life, He gives me hope of victory. That's why I love Him!

---

[1] Matthew Forney, "How Nike Figured Out China," *Time,* Oct. 25, 2004,

[2] Kenneth Strand, " 'Overcomer': A Study in the Macrodynamic of Theme Development in the Book of Revelation," *Andrews University Seminary Studies,* vol. 28, no. 3 (1990): 237-254.

[3] Bauckham, *The Theology of the Book of Revelation,* p. 69.

[4] Beale, *The Book of Revelation,* p. 312.

[5] Loren L. Johns, *The Origins and Rhetorical Force of the Lamb Christology of the Apocalypse of John* (Dissertation, Princeton Theological Seminary, 1998), p. 221.

[6] Bauckham, p. 88.

[7] Osborne, *Revelation,* pp. 225, 226.

[8] Marianne M. Thompson, "Worship in the Book of Revelation," *Ex Auditu,* vol. 8 (1992), p. 47.

[9] Osborne, p. 175.

[10] *Ibid.,* p. 112.

[11] *Ibid.,* p. 188.

[12] *Ibid.,* p. 58.

[13] Bauckham, pp. 72, 78.

[14] *Ibid.,* p. 160.

[15] Stefanovic, *Revelation of Jesus Christ,* p. 312.

[16] "For all the nations have drunk of the wine of the passion of her immorality, and the kings of the earth have committed *acts* of immorality with her, and the merchants of the earth have become rich by the wealth of her sensuality" (Rev. 18:3); "To the degree that she glorified herself and lived sensuously, to the same degree give her torment and mourning; for she says in her heart, 'I SIT *as* A QUEEN AND I AM NOT A WIDOW, and will never see mourning'" (verse 7); "And the kings of the earth, who committed *acts* of immorality and lived sensuously with her, will weep and lament over her when they see the smoke of her burning" (verse 9).

[17] Beale, p. 312.

[18] Johns, p. 221.

[19] Bauckham, p. 77; Stephanovic, pp. 159-180; Jon Paulien, "The Seven Seals," *Symposium on Revelation—Book 1,* Daniel and Revelation Committee Series 6 (Silver Spring, Md.: Biblical Research Institute, 1992), pp. 201, 202; Elizabeth Schussler Fiorenza, *Revelation: Vision of a Just World,* Proclamation Commentaries (Minneapolis: Fortress Press, 1991), p. 59.

[20] Beale, p. 312.

[21] Johns, pp. 197, 198.

[22] *Ibid.,* pp. 211, 213.

[23] Beale, p. 271.

[24] See Bauckham, p. 70.

[25] David M. May, *Revelation: Weaving a Tapestry of Hope* (Macon, Ga.: Smyth and Helwys, 2001), p. 92.

[26] Stott, *The Incomparable Christ,* p. 199.

[27] Johnson, *The Triumph of the Lamb,* p. 184; Osborne, p. 480.

[28] Stefanovic, p. 389.

[29] Beale, p. 658.

[30] *Ibid.,* pp. 658-661; Doukhan, *Secrets of Revelation,* p. 111.

[31] Osborne, p. 476.

[32] Stefanovic, p. 389.

[33] See Beale, p. 436.

[34] *Ibid.,* p. 663.

[35] *Ibid.,* p. 191.

[36] Osborne, p. 480; Bauckham, pp. 66-108.

[37] May, p. 94; Beale, pp. 666, 667.

[38] May, p. 94.

[39] Osborne, p. 34.

[40] *Ibid.,* p. 452.

[41] *Ibid.,* p. 34.

[42] May, p. 81.

[43] Forney.

[44] Beale, p. 663.

[45] *Ibid.*, p. 191.

[46] Seé *ibid.*, p. 436.

[47] Ellen G. White, *The Great Controversy,* p. 649.

[48] Robert H. Charles, *A Critical and Exegetical Commentary on the Revelation of St. John* (Edinburg: T and T Clark, 1956-1959), pp. 53, 54.

[49] Thomas, *Revelation 8-22,* p. 303.

HE FILLS MY IMAGINATION

An Eye for the Road
Revelation 5:6

I knew we were in trouble even before we drove out of Madrid's airport parking lot. It was 2:00 a.m. Our flight had arrived at midnight, and nearly an hour went by before our luggage showed up on the baggage carousel. Renting a car cost us another 40 minutes. We had Internet directions to the motel we were going to stay at somewhere north of the city, but you needed a magnifying glass to read the tiny (and sparsely detailed) map that the car rental agent had given us. As we strained to read by the car's dim map light, it wasn't clear just where we were in relation to either the map or the city. Obviously the clear Internet directions were worthless unless we knew where we were and what road we should take from the airport.

So we asked the security guard at the gate on the way out, "Where are we? Which way do we go from here? Right or left?" Blank stares. "What's the name of this road?" More blank stares. The guard didn't know English, and we didn't know Spanish. He just kept waving his arm for us to leave. So off we drove—without a good map, not knowing where we were, and not knowing the language. We had no idea whether we should turn left or right out of the parking lot. Now, I'm usually pretty good at directions, so circling Madrid for the next two hours of the very early morning was frustrating (not to mention extremely embarrassing).

More than once in my life I have wandered around unnecessarily for long periods of time on foot or in my car because I was utterly confused or lost. Not only did I waste my time, but I would sometimes arrive late or miss an important meeting altogether. Occasionally I wound up in dangerous and lonely places. Once I nearly ran into the car in front of me, because my mind was more occupied with figuring out where I was than watching where I was going. Without a good, reliable map you can get lost in very dangerous places. You can squander a great deal of time and resources. Or you may never reach your destination at all. In addition, you may endanger or hurt others by your haste and mistakes.

When you're traveling, you need an eye for the road. Besides knowing where you are and where you are going, you must have a good, reliable map or clear directions to get where you are going. It's always best to travel with someone who knows where they are (or where you are) and how to get to your destination.

This saga of maps and travel provides a helpful metaphor for life. A philosophical map—a worldview with moral and spiritual principles through which we interpret reality and make decisions—is just as essential for finding our way in life as good maps and directions are for navigating geographically. The world is full of such maps. Hollywood puts out maps that show the road of irresponsible self-indulgence as the way to happiness. (A lot of profitless wandering around and a high number of wrecks result when people use them.) Many governments now put out maps urging citizens to take the lottery road to arrive at wealth and happiness (a bald-faced lie financed with tax money). Businesses put lots of money into maps directing us onto the consumer superhighway to arrive at satisfaction. Evolution provides a map. So do the *Left Behind* novels and the slick televangelists who promise a blessing or healing when you send money. Politicians of every persuasion have their maps. Some in our postmodern age even urge us to draw our own personal itinerary. Apart from the personal dangers of living in such a fabricated dream world, there are just too many people on the road for each of us to insist on making and following our own personal maps. We need better maps than these.

The book of Revelation gives us a map of sorts: "The Revelation of Jesus Christ, which God gave Him to show to His bond-servants, the things which must soon take place; and He sent and communicated *it* by His angel to His bond-servant John" (Rev. 1:1, NASB). "And he said to me, 'These words are faithful and true; and the Lord, the God of the spirits of the prophets, sent His angel to show to His bond-servants the things which must soon take place'" (Rev. 22:6, NASB). "Therefore write the things which you have seen, and the things which are, and the things which will take place after these things" (Rev. 1:19, NASB; cf. Rev. 4:1). Revelation promises direction for the road ahead. It gives us a glimpse of what must soon take place and orients us by providing important bearings in relation to the past, present, and future ("the things which you have seen, and the things which are, and the things which will take place after these things"). Thus the book offers us a glimpse of things moral and spiritual in both history and life.

I'm not suggesting at all that Revelation gives us a detailed, step-by-step outline from A to Z that we can read along with the daily news or a history book in our hand. But it does provide a philosophical map (a worldview)[1] with some relevant historical anchor points that enable us to understand how the moral and spiritual matters it touches on fit life both in whatever moment of history we may find ourselves living in and in the epochal times before the end.

Revelation's opening verses indicate that it belongs not just to one but to three kinds of literature: apocalypse (a revealing), prophecy, and letter (Rev. 1:1, 3, 4-6; cf. Rev.22:7; 10; 18; 19).[2] In other words, it is *apocalyptic prophecy* in the form of a circular letter.[3] Thus Revelation is a unique blend of three literary genres that can fill the imagination with life-orienting truth. That combination of prophecy, letter, and apocalyptic imagery affirms the essential temporal nature of the Apocalypse. It is a book concerned with human time and history—where it is all headed and the significant moral and spiritual issues along the way. The Apocalypse reflects an incredible diversity and comprehensiveness that enables it to cast its prophetically nuanced moral and spiritual vision across all of human life, thought, and experience.

That's why I love Jesus. He gives me an eye for the road, providing life-orienting truth that can guide me along my way. To accomplish this, He sends His Holy Spirit into the world in order both to cast that apocalyptic prophetic vision and to help me understand it (Rev. 19:10; 12:17). I get excited every time I think about it!

The Spirit and the Lamb

Compared with its mentioning of God and Christ, references to the Holy Spirit in Revelation are comparatively few. But it is a mistake to conclude that the Spirit's presence is either secondary or unimportant.

The Spirit plays an essential role in the book. At Revelation's beginning we find the Spirit adjacent to the throne of God, sharing in the Trinity's promise of grace and peace (Rev. 1:4; cf. Rev. 4:5). At the book's close we hear the Spirit beckoning us to come (Rev. 22:17). Then in chapter 5, at Revelation's theological (and ethical) heart,[4] we find the Spirit closely connected to the celebrated slain Lamb: "And I saw between the throne (with the four living creatures) and the elders a Lamb standing, as if slain, having seven horns and seven eyes, which are the seven Spirits of God, sent out into all the earth" (Rev. 5:6, NASB). Most of us stop reading when we get to "a Lamb standing, as if slain." The imagery here of Jesus is awesome! So much so that we become so absorbed in its truth of His substitutionary death that we forget to read on and hear about the Spirit in relation to our great Savior. Notice the intimate association of the Spirit with the victorious Lamb. The book portrays the Lamb as having "seven horns and seven eyes, which are the seven Spirits of God, sent out into all the earth." You need to think about what you are reading. Jesus doesn't have seven horns and seven eyes in His pocket, or in a bag that He carries, as if they are external and detachable entities. Rather they are an organic part of who He is as the slain Lamb. When you see the Lamb, you see the horns and eyes. The "sevenfold Spirit" is so closely identified with Jesus that they are nearly one. Furthermore, Jesus sends the Spirit into the world, a reference to Pentecost (Acts 1:8; 2:4; 10:44).

Here John identifies the seven Spirits with both the seven horns and the seven eyes of the Lamb. It points to the Lamb's ability to see what happens throughout the world and to act powerfully wherever He chooses.[6] In Old Testament Scripture horns often represented strength and power, so seven horns suggest the fullness of divine power. Eyes point to the all-seeing nature of the Spirit. In Zechariah 4:10 the "seven eyes of the Lord" "range . . . throughout the earth" (NASB). The seven horns and the seven eyes belong to the Lamb and represent the power of His victory. The Spirit goes out into all the earth to make His victory effective everywhere.[7]

Revelation thus unfolds the Holy Spirit as our best helper—both to see and to overcome. We need the power of the Holy Spirit in our lives for witness, for honoring Jesus, and for being like Him in the world. All of us are powerless on our own. So the Godhead sends the Spirit out into the world. Jesus dispatches His Spirit to me so that I can be an overcomer and share His victory. The Spirit's presence represents the power of Christ's victory in my life and in the world.

REVELATION'S GREAT LOVE STORY

The Spirit and the Book of Revelation

The Spirit provides more, though, than the promise of strength and power for Christlike living—He gives us an eye for the road, helping us know where we are and where we're headed. I like to think of Him as someone in the back seat giving me directions as I navigate through life with the Apocalypse in hand. That's how I read those repeated exhortations to the seven churches: "He who has an ear, let him hear what the Spirit says to the churches" (Rev. 2:7, 11, 17, 29; 3:6, 13, 22, NASB).

In an earlier chapter ("In the Blink of an Ear") we learned how Jesus stands in the middle of His church speaking (Rev. 2:1, 8, 12, 18; 3:1, 7, 14). Revelation portrays Christ as walking among His gathered, listening, praying, believing, struggling, hurting, anxious, compromising, weary, and troubled people (Rev. 2:1-3:22). He always has something important to say about everything going on in our life and our world and our church.

We discovered there, too, that the last thing our great Senior Pastor spoke to every church was the command to "hear what the Spirit says to the churches" (NASB). In other words, when Jesus speaks, so does the Spirit. Whatever differences exist between the seven churches, two things remain constant: the Spirit conveys (speaks) what Jesus has to declare, and the people are to listen.[8]

Finally, we also saw how Jesus instructed John to write down everything He desired to communicate to the churches. His assignment would ultimately include the whole book of Revelation—all that John saw, not just the contents of the seven letters (Rev. 1:1-3, 11, 19; 4:1; 14:13; 19:9; 21:5; 22:7, 18, 19). What Jesus presented is not only able to be literally spoken and heard, but also written down, read, and kept (Rev. 1:3, 11; 22:6, 7, 9, 18, 19). It assumes that what Jesus has to say has understandable form, content, and, most important, meaning (Rev. 1:3; 22:9).

Putting these three thoughts together, we concluded that the written Word of Jesus (the book of Revelation) is as good as the voice of Jesus. It is just as authoritative, because through it He still speaks. A close link exists between both Jesus and the written words of Revelation and between Him and the Spirit. John was "in the spirit" when he heard and saw and was instructed to write (Rev. 1:10; 4:2; 17:3; 21:10). We can assume that the same Spirit inspired the prophet when he later actually transcribed the things that he heard and saw. Revelation is a

Spirit-inspired apocalyptic prophecy.

The Spirit and Prophecy

In his biography *American Soldier* General Tommy Franks tells how for thousands of years soldiers have longed for the power to see and understand what was happening on the battlefield as the chaos of the battle unfolded. Where is the enemy? Where are our own forces? Have we captured the objective or been pushed back? Commanders on the field call it the "fog and friction" of war—an evocative metaphor attributed to the eighteenth-century Prussian military strategist Carl von Clausewitz.[9] Franks describes the new kind of war that commanders now wage in which they can see in real time what is going on in the battlefield. GPS systems, video cameras, satellite signals and imagery, large-screen TV monitors, night-vision goggles, and computer-enhanced depiction now enable a level of communication and understanding imagined only in science-fiction movies and novels. The Iraq war brought such things together in a powerful way that leveraged information over troop numbers, speed, and tactics over fortifications and large distances.

Revelation's "Spirit of prophecy" dissipates the "fog and friction" of war. John points to this when he wrote: "And the dragon was enraged with the woman, and he went to make war with the rest of her offspring, who keep the commandments of God and have the testimony of Jesus Christ" (Rev. 12:17, NKJV). The dragon is angry with an end-time people who exhibit a lifestyle of obedience and "have the testimony of Jesus Christ." But what is the latter? Is it the Gospel? the New Testament? a modern-day prophet? the church's witness to the world or the book of Revelation or what Jesus says to His people?

Later in Revelation we receive an important clue that helps us find the answer. John has just heard a lot of noisy celebration in heaven—hallelujahs, in fact, because God has finally and fully judged the harlot city Babylon and avenged the blood of His people (Rev. 19:1-5). As loud joy ripples through heaven like the overwhelming roar of a great shouting multitude and booming peals of thunder, John hears that the "Lord God Almighty" reigns (verse 6, NIV). The great multitude announces the wedding of the Lamb with the intense expressions of joy always associated with such celebrations (verses 7, 8). The bride has adorned herself (verses 7, 8). A blessing is pronounced on those invited to the wedding banquet (verse 9). What does John do? "And I fell at his feet to worship him. But he said to me, 'See *that you do* not *do that!* I am your fellow servant, and of your brethren who have the testimony of Jesus. Worship God! For the testimony of Jesus is the spirit of prophecy' " (verse 10, NKJV). It's another one of those passages we can read in a hurry, but if we stop to look at it more carefully we learn volumes about the Spirit's work in our behalf.

The angel's forceful interruption of John's misguided worship closely links four important biblical realities: Jesus, the Spirit, prophecy, and testimony. Note, too, that one phrase interprets another—"the testimony of Jesus Christ" *is* "the spirit of prophecy." This is important, because whatever the "testimony of Jesus" is in the book of Revelation, it has something to do both with the Spirit and with prophecy. Revelation consciously links them together.

Anyone who studies the book of Revelation knows that it is Scripture's last word on Christ.[10] The book portrays Christ in a way that does not appear anywhere else in the Bible.[11] We behold a majestic, commanding, glorious, powerful Christ who is at the book's center.[12] All of Revelation is a testimony from Jesus and about Him.[13]

The Spirit is not far from this last word on Christ. In the Apocalypse the Spirit always works in close relationship with Jesus (Rev. 5:6). We would expect Him to be active wherever Christ speaks and reveals Himself. Elsewhere John tells us that the Spirit does not speak of Himself, but reveals Jesus and what He has to say to His church: "But when He, the Spirit of truth, comes, He will guide you into all the truth; for He will not speak on His own initiative, but whatever He hears, He will speak; and He will disclose to you what is to come. He will glorify Me, for He will take of Mine and will disclose *it* to you. All things that the Father has are Mine; therefore I said that He takes of Mine and will disclose *it* to you" (John 16:13-15, NASB). Did you notice that Jesus declares that the Spirit will "disclose to you what is to come"?

Prophecy is a major focus of the last book of Scripture. In fact, Revelation refers to itself as prophecy. It is a book of prophecy (Rev. 22:19) and is filled with words of prophecy (Rev. 1:3; 22:7, 10, 18). As we have seen previously, it is apocalyptic prophecy in the form of a circular letter.[14] It seems best to call Revelation an *apocalyptic prophecy*.[15] As a prophecy, Revelation was meant to be read aloud in the context of Christian worship with the intent to help its hearers understand their historical situation and to discern the divine purpose in their situation so that they could respond to it in an appropriate way.[16] The book sought to give perspective, shape moral life, and outline the future (Rev. 1:3; 22:6, 7, 18, 19).[17] That is, it shows us where we are, where we've been, and where we're going! In the process it gathers up and interprets what God had revealed to the prophets of the past into a new and finally fulfilling prophetic revelation.[18]

It is here that we that we must understand the important link between the Spirit and prophecy. It is the Spirit who initiates and empowers prophecy. Throughout Scripture the Spirit and prophecy are nearly synonymous (1 Thess. 5:19, 20; 1 Peter 1:10; Num. 11:29; 1 Sam. 10:10; 19:20; 2 Peter 1:21; 1 John 4:1). As the book of Revelation closes it mentions how "The Lord, the God of the spirits of the prophets, sent His angel to show to His bond-servants the things which must soon take place" (Rev. 22:6, NASB). The Spirit in the Apocalypse refers generally to the "spirit of prophecy" (Rev. 19:10).[19]

Finally, Revelation 19:10 intentionally connects the notion of Spirit-inspired prophecy with the "testimony of Jesus." One of the implications of such a link is that when the Spirit inspires prophecy, its content is the witness of Jesus.[20] It is the gospel.[21] And it unfolds a theodicy of God's handling of the reality of evil in the person and work of Jesus within the unfolding cosmic conflict.[22] But the "testimony of Jesus" as the "spirit of prophecy" tells us that the gospel is placed within the context of apocalyptic prophecy. This gives a context and urgency to the gospel that is both illumining and compelling. Most immediately, it is John's own prophecy, the book of Revelation (cf. Rev. 1:3; 22:7, 18, 19).[23] Four times John tells us that he was "in the Spirit" (Rev. 1:10; 4:2; 17:3; 21:10). All 14 references to the Spirit in Revelation in one way or another concern the Spirit's inspiration of John's prophecy—the book of Revelation itself.[24]

But Revelation's "the testimony of Jesus" also includes the prophetic ministry of others. The angel that John tried to worship refers to "brethren who hold the testimony of Jesus" (Rev. 19:10, NASB). On another occasion the angel became even more specific: "But he said to me, 'Do not do that. I am a fellow servant of yours and of your brethren the prophets and of those who heed the words of this book. Worship God'" (Rev. 22:9, NASB). The phrase "your brethren who hold the testimony of Jesus" is parallel with "your brethren the prophets." Those who have the testimony of Jesus are prophets inspired by the Spirit. Some commentators argue that the term *brothers* in the book of Revelation always means "prophet."[25] And that the phrase "your brothers the prophets" has the ring of a fixed idiom.[26]

Not only does this underscore our earlier link between the testimony of Jesus as being prophetic in nature—it helps us understand how Revelation is hinting at the activity of the Spirit through Christian prophets in the churches.[27] The Spirit's sphere of operation is the churches in which He inspires the ministry of Christian prophets to the rest of the community.[28] Prophecy is a witness of Jesus. It is also a "brotherhood," a sphere of giftedness to the church. The Spirit's message through prophets to the churches in every or any age is designed to prepare and to enable the churches to bear prophetic witness to the world, inspired by the Spirit.[29] When the Spirit inspires prophecy, its content is the witness of Jesus, and such witness will bring significant revelation of God's character and actions in handling the reality of evil (Rev. 15:3, 4; 16:7; 19:1-5).[30] Revelation 12:17 tells us that such will be so even to the end of time.

The book of Revelation goes even further, though. It points not just to John's prophetic book of Revelation or to the prophetic ministry of other prophets throughtout time, but to the prophetic vocation of the end-time people of God as well. In fact, the whole church in the Apocalypse is endowed with the Spirit of prophecy, so that it may bear powerful witness of Jesus in the world: "And the dragon was enraged with the woman, and he went to make war with the rest of her offspring, who keep the commandments of God and have the testimony of Jesus Christ" (Rev. 12:17, NKJV).[31] The little Greek word for "have" means more than just possessing—as when you have something in your pocket. It often refers to the essence of something as well, indicating what you are because of what you have. Putting it plainly, it simply means that in the end God's people will not only have the prophetic gift in their midst, but are in themselves a prophesying remnant. They proclaim the everlasting gospel of Jesus Christ in an apocalyptic prophetic context.[32] While specific prophets stand in the background, the vocation of prophecy extends to the church as a whole through to the end.

Let me pause here for some observations about the differences and similarities that exist between what the prophet *hears* and *sees* and what actually gets written down as *words* of prophecy for us to read (Rev. 1:2, 10, 11, 19; 22:8). The *hearing* and *seeing* of the prophet is undoubtedly the "Spirit of prophecy" dynamically at work as inspired revelation in the prophet's life, while "the testimony of Jesus" is more likely the inspired message and content of the revelation that the prophets convey through what they have both *heard* and *seen* (Rev. 1:2, 3; 22:7, 9, 10, 18, 19). According to Revelation, this *seeing* and *hearing* can be written down in concrete words and become both "words of prophecy" and a "book of prophecy" (Rev. 22:7, 9, 10, 18, 19). They are organically linked and inseparable, however, "for no prophecy was ever made by an act of human will, but men moved by the Holy Spirit spoke [or wrote] from God" (2 Peter 1:21, NASB). And all Scripture is authoritatively inspired of God, both in its reception and articulation in words (1 Tim. 3:16). John makes it very clear that Revelation is more than just what he heard and saw. It is an authoritative book of prophecy that no one has the right to add to or take away from. Furthermore, John understood that the "testimony of Jesus" is more than any prophet individually, but focuses on the message and content of the apocalyptic prophecy. It was something that the angel helped him to grasp as well (Rev. 19:10; 22:9).

The Spirit Against the Spirits

A few years back I looked into the fuel tank of my VW Rabbit diesel trying to find the in-tank filter. The engine of my car had been running rough. As I would drive along, it would suddenly slow down and then just die. Something, I guessed, was clogging the filter in the tank. Or I had some bad fuel. So I removed the back seat to take a look. Unscrewing the sealed cap, I peered inside with a flashlight. Diesel fuel is usually clear, but my tank was filled with murky cream-colored swirls. Not sure what I was looking for or where the filter might be, I played the flashlight beam around in that murky liquid. Peter tells us that prophecy is like a lamp shining in a dark place: "*So* we have the prophetic word made more sure, to which you do well to pay attention as to a lamp shining in a dark place, until the day dawns and the morning star arises in your hearts" (2 Peter 1:19, NASB). The NEB uses the expression "like a lamp shining in a murky place." Here is the function of the prophetic word: to give enlightenment to those surrounded by moral and spiritual murkiness.

Revelation emphasizes the murkiness of prophetic delusion in the last days: "And I saw coming out of the mouth of the dragon and out of the mouth of the beast and out of the mouth of the false prophet, three unclean spirits like frogs; for they are spirits of demons, performing signs, which go out to the kings of the whole world, to gather them together for the war of the great day of God, the Almighty" (Rev. 16:13, 14, NASB; cf. Rev. 13:13, 14; 19:20). The book warns of a time that false prophets will deceive the world.

Elsewhere Jesus says that "false Christs and false prophets will appear and perform great signs and miracles to deceive even the elect—if that were possible" (Matt. 24:24, NIV). In the end Satan's delusions will eventually become so subtle and powerful that only "the elect" will come through unscathed.[33] Only the "elect" will be "taken" because only they are not misled. Evidently they are a group of people who know Jesus Christ and the prophecies of the Bible so well that the devil cannot mislead them. Prophetic delusions cannot confuse them because they correctly understand Bible prophecy.

What we need to realize is that Revelation's vision of the saints' clash between the dragon and a fallen world is that of a "prophetic conflict."[34] The three angels' messages of Revelation 14:6–12 are God's prophetic media blitz against the lamblike beast's propaganda about the beast that emerges from the sea (Rev. 13).[35] And the angel of Revelation 18 who dramatically illumines a darkened world and calls for God's people to leave Babylon is in contrast to the demonic lies about reality.

Revelation pits Spirit against spirits. Prophecy against prophecy. Prophetic truth against prophetic delusion. A good reliable philosophical map against a sinisterly defective philosophical one. The book's "Spirit of prophecy" thus dissipates the "fog and friction" of war, in which one's interpretations of books such as Daniel and Revelation are so crucial.

The Spirit and the Prophetic Pysche

The dragon then is angry with an end-time people who exhibit both a lifestyle of obedience as well as a prophetic impulse. He is angry that the everlasting gospel is set in an apocalyptic prophetic context, a unique framework that brings understanding and urgency and that compels decision. The church then turns around and gives this testimony of Jesus to a confused and bewitched world, blowing the devil's deceptive cover and exposing his real motives. The dragon knows the power of apocalyptic prophecy to fully unveil Jesus.

The "testimony of Jesus" thus has broader connotations than we often think. God endows the remnant church in Revelation with the Spirit of prophecy, so that it may bear witness of Jesus in the world.[36] The last-day church finds its roots and mission in prophecy and becomes a prophesying remnant or a prophetic movement.

The impact of apocalyptic prophecy will be needed until the end—either the end of our individual lives or the conclusion of history (Rev. 12:17; 2 Peter 1:19). Jesus tells us that we will face prophetic delusions in the end. Peter urges us to pay careful attention to this prophetic word so that we can wend our way through the murky prophetic waters of last-day deceptions. Even more important, we must actively turn our minds to the prophetic word as an object of personal interest and faith. Hold on to the prophecies, Peter says. Study them diligently, spending time with them. Let them orient you to life and time.

The Spirit and My Ear

When my wife and I traveled in Germany, an invisible woman in our car kept telling me where to go. Actually my Opel Signum had a GPS navigation system in it. You just pop the program disk into the CD-player, key in the city and your destination address, and start driving. A screen in the dash has a compass and an arrow that point straight or to the left or right or at an angle, depending on which direction you need to go next. And accompanying it is the very polite, well-modulated voice.

I don't know where the invisible woman was, but I quickly got used to her voice, and certainly appreciated her directions. It was as if she sat in the back seat. She knew every turn, how far it would be till the next intersection, and even how many meters it would be until my next turn. And when I made a wrong turn, she quietly recalculated my position and gently told me either to make a U-turn or adjusted her directions accordingly.

It's nice having someone in the back seat who knows everything about the road you're on. Even better yet is having someone who can look down from way out in space and figure exactly where you are in relationship to your journey. I liked the idea that my little car was being watched over and guided. I felt cared for. It made me think of that verse in Isaiah that declares, "Your ears will hear a word behind you, 'This is the way, walk in it,' whenever you turn to the right or to the left" (Isa. 30:21, NASB).

Revelation's "spirit of prophecy" helps make the Lamb's victory effective in my life. Filling my mind with life-orienting truths, it gives me an eye for the road, providing an apocalyptic prophetic vision that can guide me along my way. Such a glimpse of what "must soon take place" provides important bearings in relation to the past, present, and future. It cuts through the fog of the spiritual moral battles that I experience and the murky darkness of deception that would lead me to dangerous places. Most of all, it gives me an awesome view of Jesus—who He is and what He is doing for me. I hear of His love and incredible victory at Calvary in my behalf. That He is coming again. That He cares and is at work in my world.

That's why I love Jesus. He wants to make sure that I know where I am, where I'm going, and what's on the horizon. He wants me to arrive safely.

"He who has an ear, let him hear what the Spirit says to the churches!" (Rev. 2:7, 11, 17, 29; 3:6, 13, 22, NASB). "Believe in the Lord your God, and you shall be established; believe His prophets, and you shall prosper"

Revelation's Great Love Story

(2 Chron. 20:20, NKJV).

---

[1] Revelation's worldview includes its representation of the human condition, its depictions of the character of God, and its portrayal of the struggle between Christ and Satan. In addition, it presents such fundamentals as an ex nihilo creation, judgment, and a moral universe.

[2] Osborne, *Revelation*, pp. 12, 13; Bauckham, *The Theology of the Book of Revelation*, pp. 1, 2.

[3] Bauckham, p. 2.

[4] Johns, *The Origins and Rhetorical Force of the Lamb Christology of the Apocalypse of John*, pp. 197, 198.

[5] Here and elsewhere Revelation portrays the Spirit as the "sevenfold Spirit" (Rev. 1:4; 3:1; 4:5). See Easley, *Revelation*, p. 26.

[6] Bauckham, p. 112.

[7] *Ibid.*

[8] Peterson, *Reversed Thunder*, p. 47.

[9] Tommy Franks with Malcolm McConnell, *American Soldier* (HarperCollins, 2004), p. 175.

[10] Peterson, p. 26.

[11] Stefanovic, *Revelation of Jesus Christ*, p. 56.

[12] Peterson, p. 28.

[13] *Ibid.*, p. 26.

[14] Bauckham, p. 2.

[15] *Ibid.*, p. 6.

[16] *Ibid.*, p. 7.

[17] Beale, pp. 184, 185.

[18] Bauckham, p. 5.

[19] Swete, *Apocalypse*, p. 310.

[20] Bauckham, p. 119.

[21] *Ibid.*

[22] Sigve K. Tonstad, *Saving God's Reputation: The Theological Function of Pistis Iesou in the Cosmic Narratives of Revelation* (New York: T and T Clark International, 2006), pp. xv, xvi, 159-193.

[23] *Ibid.*

[24] *Ibid.*, p. 115.

[25] E. Earle Ellis, *Prophecy and Hermeneutic in Early Christianity* (Grand Rapids: William B. Eerdmans, 1978), p. 23, n. 1; see also pp. 13-17.

[26] *Ibid.*, p. 17.

[27] Bauckham, p. 115.

[28] *Ibid.*, p. 118.

[29] *Ibid.*, p. 119.

[30] *Ibid.*

[31] Richard Bauckham, "The Role of the Spirit in the Apocalypse," *The Evangelical Quarterly*, 52, 2, April-June 1980, p. 75.

[32] *Ibid.*

[33] Steve Wohlberg, *Truth Left Behind* (Nampa, Idaho: Pacific Press Pub. Assn., 2001), pp. 18, 19.

[34] Bauckham, *The Theology of the Book of Revelation*, p. 120.

[35] William Johnsson, "The Saint's End-time Victory Over the Forces of Evil," *Symposium on Revelation—Book II*, p. 14.

[36] Bauckham, "The Role of the Spirit in the Apocalypse," pp. 73-75.

HE GIVES ME PURPOSE

~~Rumors~~ *[Promise] of Another World*
Revelation 22:1-7

A short story by the Spanish writer Carmen Corde tells of a young woman who gave birth to a blind son. "I don't want my child to know that he is blind," she informed family and neighbors, forbidding anyone to use such telltale words as "light," "color," and "sight." The boy grew up unaware of his disability until one day a strange girl jumped over the fence of the garden and spoiled everything by using all the forbidden words. His world shattered in the face of reality.[1]

Like the girl who brought a message from the outside, John's "revelation of Jesus Christ" brings rumors of another world beyond the fence, of an afterlife beyond death, of a loving God who is somehow working out His will in the chaotic history of our planet. As in Carmen Corde's story, the news may not always be welcome. But for me, Revelation opens my life to a horizon of meaning and purpose that I can both experience now and enjoy for all eternity. Let's read two incredible pictures of these rumors of another world:

"Then I saw a new heaven and a new earth, for the old heaven and the old earth had disappeared. And the sea was also gone. And I saw the holy city, the new Jerusalem, coming down from God out of heaven like a beautiful bride prepared for her husband. I heard a loud shout from the throne, saying, 'Look, the home of God is now among his people! He will live with them, and they will be his people. God himself will be with them. He will remove all of their sorrows, and there will be no more death or sorrow or crying or pain. For the old world and its evils are gone forever.' And the one sitting on the throne said, 'Look, I am making all things new!' And then he said to me, 'Write this down, for what I tell you is trustworthy and true.' And he also said, 'It is finished! I am the Alpha and the Omega—the Beginning and the End. To all who are thirsty I will give the springs of the water of life without charge! All who are victorious will inherit all these blessings, and I will be their God, and they will be my children'" (Rev. 21:1-7, NLT).

"And the angel showed me a pure river with the water of life, clear as crystal, flowing from the throne of God and of the Lamb, coursing down the center of the main street. On each side of the river grew a tree of life, bearing twelve crops of fruit, with a fresh crop each month. The leaves were used for medicine to heal the nations. No longer will anything be cursed. For the throne of God and of the Lamb will be there, and his servants will worship him. And they will see his face, and his name will be written on their foreheads. And there will be no night there—no need for lamps or sun—for the Lord God will shine on them. And they will reign forever and ever. Then the angel said to me, 'These words are trustworthy and true: "The Lord God, who tells his prophets what the future holds, has sent his angel to tell you what will happen soon."' 'Look, I am coming soon! Blessed are those who obey the prophecy written in this scroll'" (Rev. 22:1-7, NLT).

Here's a vision for my life that is bigger than I could ever have imagined.

Have you ever wondered, *Why on earth am I here?* Pondered the purpose, the direction, the difference your life makes—if any? Who you are? Where you're headed? Of course you have. We all have. It's the question that my father's wife, Esta, wrestles with now that Dad has died and she is alone and grieving and too often abandoned by friends who used to come by. Ninety-seven-year-old Violet Pool asked it of me dozens of time when her son Phil died and nearly all her friends were gone. Teenagers raise it as they experience puberty and transition their way from total dependence toward independence. College students wonder it when they enroll as freshmen or find themselves in their junior year with no clue whatever as to the major their school is pressing them to settle on. Retirees ask it when they transition out of the workplace that until then had given them purpose, a sense of identity, and meaning. We struggle with it when we taste the bitter root of moral failure or the boa-constricting grip of substance, sexual, or verbal abuse. Perhaps we cope with chronic medical problems or disabilities or struggle to recover from the failure of our business. The list is endless. Anything can make us question the meaning and purpose of life.

"Why on earth am I here?" can haunt our thinking at almost every moment of life. I've asked it a few times myself. What difference am I making? What should I do with my life? What purpose do I serve? Where am I going? What will the future bring?

Even in Scripture many people expressed the kind of bewilderment that underlies this question. Isaiah complained, "I have labored to no purpose; I have spent my strength in vain and for nothing" (Isa. 49:4, NIV). Job said, "My life flies by—day after hopeless day" (Job 7:6, TLB), and "I give up; I am tired of living. Leave me alone. My life makes no sense" (Job 7:16, TEV). Solomon asked it throughout Ecclesiastes in which he kept saying that life is meaningless, like mist in the air.

Once I had an extended conversation with an undercover narcotics detective working in my county. Making two or three busts a week, he would knock down doors and handcuff people after pinning them to the floor. He spoke of people living for the moment, the rush. How getting caught did not faze them. Having learned the system, they knew that they would do some time if caught, but the rush seemed worth the hassle. The detective described people living in houses filled with human feces and trash everywhere. While they would have an Xbox or PlayStation, big-screen TVs, and dozens of new $100 shoes or expensive leather jackets, they wouldn't invest a dime in the house itself. If you or I had someone hold a gun to our heads, our eyes would bug out. But not these guys.

The greatest tragedy is not death or difficulties or suffering, but life without purpose, of living for the thrill of the moment, which is just that—a moment.

The book of Revelation gives me a goal for living. It's about living on purpose—the reason I'm here. Jesus has things in mind for me that are bigger than I ever imagined. That's why I love Him!

Living Water

Christ's first purpose is for me to know Him personally and to drink from the water of life even as I live each day right now: "Then He said to me, 'It is done. I am the Alpha and the Omega, the beginning and the end. I will give to the one who thirsts from the spring of the water of life without cost'" (Rev. 21:6, NASB). "Then he showed me a river of the water of life, clear as crystal, coming from the throne of God and of the Lamb, in the middle of its street. On either side of the river was the tree of life" (Rev. 22:1, NASB).

While this will be a future experience for sure, Revelation also assumes that I can drink of such living water even now: "The Spirit and the bride say, 'Come.' And let the one who hears say, 'Come.' And let the one who is thirsty come; let the one who wishes take the water of life without cost" (verse 17, NASB). Although the language is of the river of life found in the New Jerusalem (verse 1), one may now, at any time during earthly life, take the free gift of the water of life (Isa. 55:1). Although we will not fully enjoy the glories of heaven until the consummation, yet every person who hears and comes to Jesus will begin experiencing heavenly benefits immediately (Heb. 6:4, 5).[2] This mirrors Christ's invitation elsewhere in John's writings that present salvation as a present reality: "But whoever drinks of the water that I will give him shall never thirst; but the water that I will give him will become in him a well of water springing up to eternal life" (John 4:14, NASB). "Jesus stood and cried out, saying, 'If anyone is thirsty, let him come to Me and drink. He who believes in Me, as the Scripture said, "From his innermost being will flow rivers of living water."' But this He spoke of the Spirit, whom those who believed in Him were to receive; for the Spirit was not yet given, because Jesus was not yet glorified" (John 7:37-39, NASB).

The invitation to "come" is without question the most evangelistic text in the entire book of Revelation. Here we find a gracious and wide invitation to experience joy and salvation that follows a graphic picture of gloom and despair for the lost. Jesus invites all those in the seven churches to avail themselves of this free offer. The door of mercy still open, He calls out to the thirsty. Ultimately, many will refuse to come. Now, however, opportunity remains for the world's inhabitants to come to Christ.

So Revelation promises me release from my sins through Christ's blood (Rev. 1:5). In fact, I can immerse my character and life in His blood and be freed from both the penalty and power of sin (Rev. 7:14; 22:14; 12:11; 20:11-15). I can have peace, assurance, hope, and a new life in Christ that enables me to overcome in those important areas that really matter both now and in eternity.

Worthy of My Everything

Christ's second purpose for me is to live wholeheartedly for Him— honoring Him in everything I am and in everything I do. He wants me to make the most of all that I am and all that I have for Him: "And the throne of God and of the Lamb will be in it, and His bond-servants will serve Him" (Rev. 22:3, NASB). John here writes of bond-servants who serve the Lamb. We find a similar picture of the redeemed who "are before the throne of God; and they serve Him day and night in His temple" (Rev. 7:15). Why do they hang around the throne and serve God day and night? Is it forced labor? Even the Greek word for "bond-servants" means *slaves*. The primary emphasis is on the whole of one's life as sacrificial worship surrendered to God, as we read in Romans: "In view of God's mercy, . . . offer your bodies as living sacrifices . . . this is your spiritual act of worship" (Rom. 12:1, NIV). After all, those who serve before the throne have come out of great tribulation. Having washed their robes and made them white in the Lamb's blood, they stand before the throne with palm branches of victory in their hands. They are full of songs of redemption (Rev. 7:9, 10, 13, 14). Oh, how they sing. Filled with awe, they give God and the Lamb full credit for their great salvation.

It makes me think of Paul's words to the Corinthians: "The love of Christ compels me. It controls me. It completely dominates me, hems me in. Propels me" (see 2 Cor. 5:14, 15). When you visit Ontario's Agawa Rock—where nearly 400 years ago the Ojibwa people painted red ocher figures on sheer cliff walls that slide down into Lake Superior—the 15-minute walk down from the parking lot takes you unexpectedly through a crevasse. You suddenly find yourself walking in the middle of what seems like a colossal boulder that has split in half. Eventually the path narrows to barely 30 inches wide. For the next 100 or so feet you see nothing to the left and nothing to the right but solid rock walls reaching to the heavens. Only a narrow sliver of sky is visible overhead and a narrow slit of the trail ahead, leaving you both amazed and constrained. You feel exhilarated and very small at the same time. There's only one way to go—straight ahead.

One of the family vacation pictures I cherish is a picture of the Lichtenwalters hanging on for dear life, grins as big as can be, water spraying all around, as they white-water raft in Canada's Rocky Mountains. We did it two days in a row. I've often wondered what it would be like to shoot the Colorado River rapids, down through those deep raging gorges. Solid rock walls reach to the heavens, and you can hardly turn to the right or left as raging white water propels you along. The river has a current that you cannot swim against. Once you commit yourself to it, there's no stopping or turning around. The powerful force of water rushes you along in one clearly defined direction. Not only do walls hem you in, you are driven by a force that you cannot resist.

That's the kind of imagery we find in Paul's words to the Corinthian believers explaining why he does what he does: "For the love of Christ compels us" (verse 14, NKJV). The Greek word *sunecho* means "to surround, hem in, encircle, control, constrain." Christ's love hems us in like great walls looming up toward the blue sky so that we can't go to the left or to the right. His love propels us forward like powerful surging water in a narrow channel so that you cannot remain where you are. It is love that encapsulates our very life—all that we are and all that we have. Such love produces a radical prioritizing of life—guiding it in just one direction, creating just one focus and passion. All can clearly see our passion for Jesus Christ because of what we do with whom we are and with what we have.

That's how Revelation pictures the redeemed—as slaves of God and the Lamb. What else could they ever do after all that Jesus has done for them? The innumerable angels, amazed at what the Lamb has done both for them and our little lost world, put it well: "Worthy is the Lamb that was slain to receive power and riches and wisdom and might and honor and glory and blessing" (Rev. 5:12, NASB). Yes, Jesus is worthy. Worthy of it all. Worthy of my all. Worthy of any power and strength I have for Him and His work in the world. Worthy of my praise for any blessing I ever experience. Jesus is worthy too, of my open confession of Him even if it means my very life (Rev. 12:11). Surely, after all that He has done for me, He is worthy of my perseverance in keeping His commandments and my faith in Him (Rev. 14:12; cf. Rev. 12:17).

A Vietnamese girl during the Vietnam War found herself confronted with what it meant to live for Christ. North Vietnamese Communist guerrillas overran her small Christian village. Realizing the village was Christian, the atheist guerrilla leader made everyone assemble at the small hut where the villagers held religious services. One by one he made the people stand before him. "Spit on this picture of Christ or die," he shouted, pistol in hand, his troops standing around, their own weapons locked and loaded. One after another the trembling citizens of that small village stepped forward and dutifully spit on the face of Jesus. Then she came. Hardly 9, she had watched the whole village, including her parents, deny Christ. For a moment she held the picture of Jesus in her hands as impatient voices urged her on. But she couldn't do it. Looking into the jeering face of the guerrilla leader, she said with the soft voice of a child, "After all that Jesus has done for me, how can I spit in His face?" A moment of shocked silence hung in the air, pricking every onlooker's conscience. Everyone fully expected a gunshot to her head. "Let her go, and kill all the rest," the Communist leader finally commanded. "She's the only real Christian here. She can live."

Healing the Nations *i*

Ours is a world of brokenness and alienation. Wherever we turn we find people groups at war with one another: vicious cultural, ethnic, and racial strife. Like swollen rivers, frustration, anger, hate, and violence overflows in Ireland, the Balkans, the Middle East, Berlin, Los Angeles, Baghdad. Blood flows like water because of politics, ideology, religion, some long-held hurt, or the passion for power or wealth or control. Some struggles have spanned generations, even centuries. The earth world has witnessed genocide, crusades, ethnic cleansing, holocaust, segregation, apartheid, and terrorism.

A man who left Sarajevo before the war in 1992 and joined the Serbian army that shelled the city commented during a phone conversation with his best friend, who had remained and who had had his apartment destroyed by a shell: "There's no choice. Either us or them." He meant, of course, "Either we inhabit this place or they will; either we will destroy them or they will destroy us. No other option exists."[3] One of the most distressing stories from the war in former Yugoslavia comes from a Muslim woman.

"I am a Muslim, and I am 35 years old. To my second son who was just born, I gave the name 'Jihad.' So he would not forget the testament of his mother—revenge. The first time I put my baby at my breast, I told him, 'May this milk choke you if you forget.' So be it. The Serbs taught me to hate. For the past two months there was nothing in my heart. No pain, no bitterness. Only hatred. I taught these children to love. I did. I am a teacher of literature. I was born in Ilijaš and I almost died there. My student Zoran, the only son of my neighbor, urinated into my mouth. As the bearded hooligans standing around laughed, he told me, 'You are good for nothing else, you stinking Muslim woman . . .' I do not know whether I first heard the cry or felt the blow. My former colleague, a teacher of physics, was yelling like mad, 'Ustasha, Ustasha . . .' and kept hitting me. Wherever he could. I have become insensitive to pain. But my soul? It hurts. I taught them to love, and all the while they were making preparations to destroy everything that is not of the Orthodox faith. Jihad—was. This is the only way . . ."[4]

REVELATION'S GREAT LOVE STORY

How many mothers in Bosnia or Palestine or Rwanda have sworn to teach their children hate and revenge? How many little Muslims, Serbs, Christians, Jews, Croats, Tutsis, or Hindus will grow up listening to such stories and learn such lessons—where war, revenge, and hate are not just inscribed in their names, but in their hearts?

In a world of differences—nations, tribes, languages, and people; rich and poor, slave and free, small and great (Rev. 5:9; 7:9; 10:11; 11:9; 11:18; 13:7, 16; 14:6; 17:15; 19:5, 18; cf. Gal. 3:28; Col 3:11)—God seeks healing and reconciliation between alienated hearts and hurting memories. Revelation gives me an incredible vision of this reconciliation and compels me into helping it happen: "On either side of the river was the tree of life, bearing twelve *kinds of* fruit, yielding its fruit every month; and the leaves of the tree were for the healing of the nations" (Rev. 22:2, NASB). The context suggests that God accounts for the wounds of the past.[5] Such healing is both individual and relational. Here humanity finds both blessing and final reconciliation, for "the leaves [of the tree of life] were used for medicine to heal the nations" (verse 2, NLT).[6] The rumor of another world promises that all national and linguistic barriers and alienation will be forever removed. Humanity will then be united in one family, at peace with one another and God. No greater statement of the end of one kind of moral existence and the beginning of a new one can be found in Scripture.[7]

Revelation's image of the innumerable redeemed is that they are from "every nation and *all* tribes and peoples and tongues" (Rev. 7:9, NASB). Together, and triumphant, they stand before the throne and before the Lamb, clothed in white robes, palm branches in their hands. As one they sing their hearts out: "Salvation to our God who sits on the throne, and to the Lamb" (verse 10, NASB).

But how does that happen? How do the alienated and warring peoples of all ages come together in worship, reconciled with both God and one another? Revelation maintains that it is because of the self-giving and self-sacrifice of the slain Lamb: "And they sang a new song, saying, 'Worthy are You to take the book and to break its seals; for You were slain, and purchased for God with Your blood men from every tribe and tongue and people and nation. You have made them to be a kingdom and priests to our God; and they will reign upon the earth'" (Rev. 5:9, 10, NASB). The nations are reconciled to (purchased by) God and become a new united people (a kingdom) through the Lamb's blood.

The open arms of Christ on the cross are a sign that God does not want to be alienated from us. So He suffers our violence in order to embrace us. "For if, when we were God's enemies," Paul writes, "we were reconciled to him through the death of his Son, how much more, having been reconciled, shall we be saved through his life! Not only is this so, but we also rejoice in God through our Lord Jesus Christ, through whom we have now received reconciliation" (Rom. 5:10, 11, NIV). "God was in Christ reconciling the world to Himself, not counting their trespasses against them" (2 Cor. 5:19, NASB).

Revelation affirms how Christ's self-giving and self-sacrifice has moral power to break down barriers between God and human beings and between human being and human being. The death of Christ shatters the wall of hostility that separates peoples. It enables an entirely new kingdom to form from every people group (Rev. 5:9, 10). In Christ we become one people—a new people (Rev. 1:5, 6; 5:9, 10; Eph. 2:14-18). "There is no longer Jew or Gentile, slave or free, male or female. For you are all Christians—you are one in Christ" (Gal. 3:28, NLT). The message of all Scripture, including the book of Revelation, is that the way of the Lamb becomes our way with one another.

Here is an important (and often overlooked) facet of the everlasting gospel that must be presented to "those who live on the earth, and to every nation and tribe and tongue and people" (Rev. 14:6). It is the preaching of this everlasting gospel that enables God's dream of reconciliation. Revelation's setting of the gospel in an apocalyptic prophetic context envisions divine healing of the nations. Whenever I attend General Conference sessions I catch a glimpse of God's great agenda—the rumor of another world. There I look out at the sea of ethnically diverse faces in the large auditorium and listen to the unique world division reports (and how some span scores of people groups). And I watch the parade of nations. It amazes me what Jesus has done to heal human brokenness and alienation. How He brings us together in spite of our differences. I stand in awe at the unifying power of Revelation's everlasting gospel and the biblical truths that frame its proclamation (judgment, worship, Second Coming, sanctuary, Sabbath, Creation, the nature of human beings and life, the fall of Babylon, warning against the beast, etc.).

But where do I fit into all this? What purpose should drive my soul when this kind of vision stirs my imagination? Not only does Jesus want me to be reconciled to the Father—He seeks for me to be reconciled to those with whom I may be alienated from. Jesus longs for me to open my arms as He did and embrace my enemy. His dream is for me to embrace those different from me, whether bigger or smaller, richer or poorer, slave or free, no matter what their language, culture, ethnicity, or nation. As part of His new community, the church, I will reflect the forgiveness and reconciliation that define God's nature. And He wants me to join Him in reconciling a world to Himself and its people to one another. He calls me to be His ambassador in the world. This is the message He has given me to tell others. And here is His third purpose for me.

Revelation depicts rescued people commissioned for service. God redeems for a purpose. His saving initiative in the world comes through those whom He redeems. The whole world, as a kingdom of priests, has a role to play: "To Him who loves us and released us from our sins by His blood—and He has made us to be a kingdom, priests to His God and Father" (Rev. 1:5, 6, NASB). This mission motif pulsates throughout the book. After John eats the little book that makes him sick, the angel tells him, "You must prophesy again concerning many peoples and nations and tongues and kings" (Rev. 10:11, NASB). That commissioning is followed in chapter 11 by two witnesses who unfold the fortunes of God's Word and those who preach it.[8] Then three flying angels appear in midheaven with a gospel call to a judgment-bound world (Rev. 14:6-12). Later a mighty angel descends from heaven and illumines the earth with his glory, both rebuking Babylon and inviting people to leave her (Rev. 18:4). Finally Revelation closes with the appeal to come while there is still time to take the water of life (Rev. 22:11, 17). In keeping with the rest of the New Testament, Revelation sees the church as a new exodus community fulfilling the high-priestly role of the Old Testament people of God.[9]

God has world mission in view (Rev. 14:6). The book of Revelation reminds us that the whole world is His. God loves our world (Rev. 1:5; John 3:16). He carries it on His heart and wants to heal its nations. And so must I. When the Spirit and the bride say, "Come," I am to join my voice in that heavenly invitation (Rev. 22:17).

What better purpose could I ever have in my life than to join Jesus in His great work of healing and reconciliation?

An Unshakable Life

The British novelist and playwright David Lodge was watching one of his own creations, a satirical revue, the evening of November 22, 1963. The theater audience chuckled as an actor in the play showed up for a job interview with a transistor radio clutched to his ear, demonstrating his character's blasé indifference. The actor then set down the radio and turned to a station, letting its news, music, or commercials play in the background while the play went on. This night, however, a voice on the radio broke in with a live news bulletin: "Today, the American president John F. Kennedy was assassinated . . ."

The audience gasped. The actor immediately switched off the radio, but too late. In one sentence the reality of the outside world had shattered the artificial world of the theater production. Suddenly, whatever action took place onstage seemed superficial and irrelevant.[10]

The City of God and the cities of our world exist in parallel universes (from our perspective, at least). Our problem is that we feel completely at home on earth, often unaware of another world. Like the people of the theater, we live inside a reality so engaging that we can forget about any other.

Jesus seeks to interrupt that spell by pulling our vision toward His Eternal City, and toward eternity—which has no death or curse or sorrow or sin, sinner, falsehood, or evil (Rev. 21:4, 8, 27; 22:15). Our Savior has a purpose for my life here on earth, but it doesn't end with us, and it doesn't end here. Our purpose fits into a much larger, cosmic scheme that He has designed for us individually, for His church, for our lost world, and for eternity. He wants us to grasp a sense of what we are meant to be. Solomon tells us in Ecclesiastes that God has planted eternity in the human heart (Eccl. 3:11). We have an inborn instinct that longs for immortality. Abraham Lincoln understood that reality when he wrote: "Surely God would not have created such a being as man . . . to exist only for a day! No, no, man was made for immortality." And Revelation confirms that!

This life is not all there is. When we fully comprehend that there exists more to life than just the here and now, we will begin to live differently. As we live in the light of eternity, aware of the larger picture that God has for us, our values will change. We use our time and money in more important ways. Measured against eternity, our time on earth is just a blink of an eye, but the consequences of it will last forever.

A man from northern California phoned me one day just to hear my voice. He and a small group of senior citizens had been reading my books and using them as a springboard to study God's Word together. Deeply moved by some of the things I had written, he decided to call. So there we were on the phone together even though total strangers. "Sure would like to meet you," he said in a gentle voice. I didn't detect any idolizing attitude, as if I were a great celebrity and he would get some kind of spiritual or emotional high because he got to talk with me personally. Instead, he just spoke of the things that he and others were learning about Jesus, how he was growing in the Word, and how he wanted to thank me for the part I played in his journey with Christ.

When I hung up, I couldn't help thinking of Jesus. Here had been someone who calls me and wants to meet me someday simply because I had helped him in some small way with his spiritual journey. *After all Jesus has done for me*, I said to myself, *shouldn't I have an even greater desire to see Him?* Revelation tells me that I can and that I will. I will see His face (Rev. 22:4). How many times have you longed to look upon the One you've believed in and trusted? The One who has released you from your sins, forgiven you, helped you win, and given you reason for being? Peter tells us that we can love the unseen Christ (1 Peter 1:8), but Revelation tells us that someday very soon, we will in fact see Him whom we have grown to love and follow. If we have inexpressible joy at loving Him when unseen, what will it be like when we meet Him face to face?

Revelation tells us that His name will be in our forehead. Jesus will be constantly in our thoughts. We will be like Him in character and life through all eternity.

The book of Revelation concludes its vision of eternity with a promise: "And he said to me, 'These words are faithful and true'; and the Lord, the God of the spirits of the prophets, sent His angel to show to His bond-servants the things which must soon take place. 'And behold, I am coming quickly. Blessed is he who heeds the words of the prophecy of this book'" (Rev. 22:6, 7, NASB). All this is worth living for, worth building your life around, because it's true! The words of Revelation are faithful and true. In the Apocalypse the Lord of the covenant is a God of promise. His promises are secured in His being (Rev. 1:4, 8, 17; 21:6; 22:13).[11] Faithfulness is His very character (Rev. 1:5; 3:14; 19:11; 21:5; 22:6; cf. Ps. 89:8; 138:2). Ultimately, then, it is Jesus who is firm, steadfast, unassailable, and unfaltering. He alone can be the unshakable center for my life, and because of that, I can have an unshakable life now.

The writer William Irwin Thompson likens people who cannot see past the surface to flies crawling across Michelangelo's frescoes on the ceiling of the Sistine Chapel. They are unaware of the magnificent shapes and forms that lie beneath—or above—the threshold of their perception. Even as a human being standing there on the floor looking up, you cannot take it all in at once. In fact, staring up at the frescoes for any length of time can even make you dizzy.

Jesus has a vision for my life that is bigger than I could ever imagine.

More than I can take in. In fact, almost dizzying. That's why I love Him!

Once I sat in the home of someone who told me that they were not sure there was any more hope for them. I surprised them by saying that the issue was not whether there was any hope left for him, but whether or not he would believe there was hope and reach for it through Jesus Christ. "The Spirit and the bride say, 'Come!' "

---

[1] Carmen Corde, cited in Henri Nouwren, *Gracias!* (Maryknoll, N. Y.: Orbis, 1983), p. 74.

[2] Easley, *Revelation,* p. 423.

[3] Moroslav Volf, *Exclusion and Embrace: A Theological Exploration of Identity, Otherness, and Reconciliation* (Nashville: Abingdon Press, 1996), p. 99.

[4] Zeljko Vukovic, *The Killing of Sarajevo* (Beograd: Kron, 1993), p. 134; as found in Volf, p. 111.

[5] Doukhan, *Secrets of Revelation,* p. 194.

[6] Stefanovic, *Revelation of Jesus Christ,* on Rev. 22:3.

[7] Easley, p. 395.

[8] Revelation's subtle play on words lead us to the second profound image—the two witnesses who prophecy for 1260 days clothed in sackcloth (Rev. 11:3-13). The two witnesses of Revelation 11 are the Old and New Testaments—as Ellen White asserts in *The Great Controversy* (p. 267) and Ekkehardt Muller demonstrates exegetically and theologically in his article "The Two Witnesses of Revelation 11." Muller declares that "when connected with Revelation 10 and the prophesying role of the Church . . . the imagery of the Two Witnesses in Revelation merges in that the Church becomes the context in which Scripture gives its testimony to the world . . . the Church is the mouth of the two witnesses . . . when Scripture is persecuted, those who put their trust in it are persecuted . . . the people of God experience the fortunes of the Word of God as they proclaim it fearlessly to a rebellious and lost world" (see Ekkehardt Muller, "The Two Witnesses of Revelation 11," *Journal of the Adventist Theological Society* 13/2 (Autumn 2002): pp. 30-45.

[9] Osborne, *Revelation,* p. 65.

[10] As told by Philip Yancey, *Rumors of Another World,* pp. 228, 229.

[11] Gerhard F. Hasel and Michael G. Hasel, *The Promise: God's Everlasting Covenant* (Nampa, Idaho: Pacific Press Pub. Assn., 2002), p. 48.

CONCLUSION

More Than I Ever Imagined

The book of Revelation is about loving Jesus! We don't normally (or naturally) think about the love of Jesus or of loving Him when we read the book. So many other things in it grab our attention or turn us away altogether. Nevertheless, Scripture's last word on Christ tells us about His incredible love for us and about the very close, decided connection that exists between Him and His people—including me. As I read Revelation I find many reasons for loving Him.

> I love Jesus because He's bigger than I am.
> I love Jesus because He cancels my spiritual debts.
> I love Jesus because He knows my name.
> I love Jesus because He's busy in my world.
> I love Jesus because He talks to me.
> I love Jesus because He knows everything about me.
> I love Jesus because He helps me win.
> I love Jesus because He fills my mind with life-orienting truths.
> I love Jesus because He gives me purpose for living.

In fact, Revelation's Jesus is more than I ever imagined Him to be. That means that if I keep reading this last book of Scripture, my love for Him will just grow stronger and deeper. Already my mind races ahead with themes hardly touched on or not even considered in this short volume. I could add some more chapters, but I'll let your imagination soar with the implications:

I love Jesus because He takes away my fear of death.
I love Jesus because He treats me fairly.
I love Jesus because He makes my prayers effective.
I love Jesus because He intercedes for me.
I love Jesus because He can make something out of nothing.
I love Jesus because He won't let me become lukewarm.
I love Jesus because He won't let me compromise.
I love Jesus because He will bring an end to the suffering of my world.
I love Jesus because He will vindicate me.
I love Jesus because He's coming again—soon!
I love Jesus because He offers me grace and peace.
I love Jesus because . . .
I love Jesus!

That's how my heart responds to the Revelation of Jesus Christ. What else can I do when I see Him the way John does? How could I ever forget Him or turn away from Him?
I love Jesus!